D0278098

'The Gambler' from Holbein's *Dance of Death* (see p. vii)

# THE PARDONER'S PROLOGUE & TALE

FROM THE CANTERBURY TALES

BY

## GEOFFREY CHAUCER

*Revised Edition edited with Introduction, Notes and Glossary by*

A. C. SPEARING

CAMBRIDGE
UNIVERSITY PRESS

CAMBRIDGE UNIVERSITY PRESS

Cambridge, New York, Melbourne, Madrid, Cape Town, Singapore, São Paulo, Delhi, Dubai, Tokyo

Cambridge University Press
The Edinburgh Building, Cambridge CB2 8RU, UK

www.cambridge.org
Information on this title: www.cambridge.org/9780521468183

First published 1965
17th printing 1993
Revised edition 1994
25th printing 2009

Printed in the United Kingdom at the University Press, Cambridge

*A catalogue record for this publication is available from the British Library*

ISBN 978-0-521-46818-3 paperback

The cover illustration shows a manuscript illumination depicting Geoffrey Chaucer, reproduced by permission of the Huntington Library, San Marino, California

# CONTENTS

*Frontispiece*

*Preface*                                          *page* vii

Introduction                                          1

Note on the Text                                     51

Text

   THE PORTRAIT OF THE PARDONER
   (*The General Prologue*, lines 671–716)          53

   THE INTRODUCTION TO THE
   PARDONER'S TALE                                55

   THE PARDONER'S PROLOGUE                        57

   THE PARDONER'S TALE                            63

Notes                                                79

Glossary                                             94

## *Note on the Frontispiece*

The frontispiece is taken from Hans Holbein's *Dance of Death* (ed. J. M. Clark; Phaidon Press, London, 1947. Reproduced by courtesy of the Phaidon Press). It shows three gamblers, one of whom is being seized by Death and a devil. The plate is considerably later in date than *The Pardoner's Tale*; the motif of the Dance of Death is not known until the fifteenth century, and Holbein's version of it dates from the early sixteenth century. But it remains medieval in feeling, and this plate is extraordinarily close to the Tale in subject and in its restless violence of treatment.

# PREFACE

This edition of *The Pardoner's Prologue and Tale* was first published in 1965, and has continued to be reprinted, with only minor corrections, since then. Chaucer studies have developed considerably in the last thirty years; my own view of the poem has not changed radically, but for this revised edition I have modified the Introduction considerably, giving more weight to the attitudes and practices of the medieval Church and less to the Pardoner as an individual. Some relatively small changes have also been made in the Notes and the Glossary, but the text of the Tale remains unchanged.

On medieval pardoners and medieval preaching I have borrowed without detailed acknowledgment from Alan J. Fletcher, 'The Preaching of the Pardoner', *Studies in the Age of Chaucer*, 11 (1989); J. J. Jusserand, 'Chaucer's Pardoner and the Pope's Pardoners' in *Essays on Chaucer* (Chaucer Society, 1889); Alfred L. Kellogg and Louis A. Haselmayer, 'Chaucer's Satire of the Pardoner', in Alfred L. Kellogg, *Chaucer, Langland, Arthur: Essays in Middle English Literature* (Rutgers University Press, 1972); Alastair Minnis, 'Chaucer's Pardoner and the "Office of Preacher"', in *Intellectuals and Writers in Fourteenth-Century Europe*, ed. Piero Boitani and Anna Torti (D. S. Brewer, 1986); and Arnold Williams, 'Some Documents on English Pardoners', in *Mediaeval Studies in Honor of U. T. Holmes*, ed. John Mahoney and J. E. Keller (University of North Carolina Press, 1965).

In addition to works mentioned in footnotes, readers may find the following helpful:

Piero Boitani and Jill Mann (eds.), *The Cambridge Chaucer Companion* (Cambridge University Press, 1986)

Helen Cooper, *Oxford Guides to Chaucer: The Canterbury Tales* (Clarendon Press, 1989)

Donald R. Howard, *The Idea of the Canterbury Tales* (University of California Press, 1976)

Stephan A. Khinoy, 'Inside Chaucer's Pardoner?', *Chaucer Review*, 6 (1971–2)

Peggy Knapp, *Chaucer and the Social Contest* (Routledge, New York, 1990)

David Lawton, *Chaucer's Narrators* (D. S. Brewer, 1985)

H. Marshall Leicester, *The Disenchanted Self: Representing the Subject in the Canterbury Tales* (University of California Press, 1990)

Malcolm Pittock, '*The Pardoner's Tale* and the Quest for Death', *Essays in Criticism*, 24 (1974)

Miri Rubin, *Corpus Christi: The Eucharist in Late Medieval Culture* (Cambridge University Press, 1991)

Martin Stevens and Kathleen Falvey, 'Substance, Accident, and Transformations: A Reading of the *Pardoner's Tale*', *Chaucer Review*, 17 (1982–3)

A. C. S.

*Wattlefield, Norfolk*
*August 1993*

# INTRODUCTION

*The Pardoner's Tale* is among those of the *Canterbury Tales* that have most often been extracted from the whole work and printed separately. It is right that this should be so, for it is certainly one of the finest of the *Canterbury Tales* and one of Chaucer's greatest works. The story itself, of three revellers who set out to kill Death and end by killing each other, is not original; nor are most of Chaucer's stories. This one is based on a folk-tale, of oriental origin, which has been found in various versions all over Europe. But it is told with shattering intensity, and the emotion it arouses helps to convey a profound significance. It is turned into a story of damnation, in which we see the actors not simply judged by an outraged deity, but recklessly damning themselves, throwing themselves headlong upon their fate. It is difficult to think of another work in medieval English literature in which the actual *process* of damnation is presented with such horrifying force.

Much of this force, and much of the individual colouring of the actual tale, is drawn from its teller. Nearly all of the tales told on the pilgrimage to Canterbury are related to their tellers in some way. Sometimes this is only a matter of general appropriateness, as with the Knight's chivalric romance, the Second Nun's saint's legend, or the Nun's Priest's delightful beast-fable. In other cases there is a closer relationship, so that the teller is hardly separable from the tale and its surrounding material. This is true of the Wife of Bath (whose Prologue is over twice as long as her Tale), and perhaps especially of the Pardoner. Here there are such close connections among the portrait in *The*

*General Prologue*, the Pardoner's intervention in *The Wife of Bath's Prologue*, his own Prologue, and his Tale and its aftermath, as to indicate clearly the existence of a single underlying Chaucerian conception. Even here, though, we should not think in terms of modern notions of the dramatic monologue, in which every word reveals a complex but consistent personality. The medieval tendency is to see stories as having an autonomous existence, much like natural objects, and to locate meanings in stories themselves rather than in the imagined consciousnesses of those who tell them. In *The Canterbury Tales* Chaucer was moving towards a closer connection between narrative and narratorial consciousness, and there is nothing to stop us from wondering, if we choose, what *The Pardoner's Tale* would reveal about the Pardoner if we were to imagine it as his dream. On the other hand, there is little to encourage us to hear in the Tale the distinctive 'voys . . . as smal as hath a goot' (*GP* 690) mentioned in *The General Prologue*, and the dramatic effect of 'And lo, sires, thus I preche' (629) depends on our having become so absorbed in the story as to forget temporarily the teller and his profession. There are, though, important links, to be discussed later in this Introduction, between the Pardoner's blasphemously self-destructive and damnable way of life and the themes of self-destruction, blasphemy and damnation in his Tale.

This way of life, as represented by Chaucer, is set firmly in the everyday world. The abuses of late-medieval religion are shown as they were really seen by contemporaries, only with a poet's penetration into the human experience that lies behind historical documents. The setting is everyday in another sense, too. The Tale is dramatically related to the pilgrimage: it begins with an altercation among the pilgrims and comes to an end with another altercation. We are led from this world to the very brink of the next and then brought safely back. *The Pardoner's Tale* is a work of Chaucer's high maturity, dating probably from the last decade of his life, the 1390s, and undoubtedly written specifically for inclusion in *The Canterbury Tales* and for the Pardoner to tell. It shows Chaucer's poetic art at its height, extending itself under the urgent pressure of experience to a superb virtuosity.

In this Introduction, after a brief summary of the work's content, we shall be concerned first with the Pardoner and his historical background, and then, in order, with his Prologue, Tale and conclusion.

## SUMMARY

| | |
|---|---|
| 1–42 | The Host comments on the Physician's Tale and asks the Pardoner to tell the next. He agrees to tell a 'moral' tale. |
| 43–167 | The Pardoner demonstrates to the pilgrims his methods of preaching to ignorant people, and asserts that he preaches not for their salvation but for his own gain. |
| 168–176 | He asserts that, though 'vicious' himself, he can tell a moral tale, and promises to do so, but pauses first to take a drink at a tavern. |
| 177–196 | The Tale begins. There were some young people in Flanders who used to drink and blaspheme in a tavern. |
| 197–211 | He breaks off the Tale to preach against the |

debauchees' vices. First he deals with drunkenness.

212–262    Then gluttony.

263–302    Drunkenness again, illustrated by the *exempla* of Attila and Lemuel.

303–342    He preaches against gambling, illustrated by the *exempla* of 'Stilboun' and Demetrius.

343–374    He preaches against swearing.

375–424    Return to the Tale. Three of the debauchees hear a corpse being carried past the tavern—that of a friend who has been killed by Death. They swear to seek out Death and kill him.

425–481    They meet an old man, who says that he wishes to die but cannot, and directs them down a crooked path to Death.

482–519    They find a heap of gold coins, and the 'worst' of them proposes that they should draw lots to decide which of them should go and fetch provisions, so that they can stay there till night and then carry away the gold in secret. The lot falls on the youngest, who departs for the town.

520–550    In his absence, one of the remaining two suggests to the other that they should kill the youngest on his return, and then split the gold between the two of them.

551–592    Meanwhile, the youngest decides to kill the other two, buys some poison from an apothecary, borrows some bottles, and puts the poison in two of them, filling the third with drink for himself. He returns to the gold.

593–608    The two others kill him, and then drink from

one of the bottles of poison, and so die themselves.

609–632  The Pardoner exclaims against the sins, and
continues his demonstration of how he
preaches for gain.

633–682  He turns to the pilgrims and invites them to
make offerings in return for his absolution. The
Host ought to begin. The Host rudely refuses,
and insults the Pardoner, but the Knight makes
them kiss, and the pilgrims ride on.

## THE PARDONER

We first meet the Pardoner long before he begins on his
Tale, in *The General Prologue* to *The Canterbury Tales*.
There the 'nine-and-twenty' men and women who gather
together at the Tabard Inn in Southwark before setting off
on their pilgrimage to the shrine of St Thomas à Becket at
Canterbury are described at varying lengths. Some are
dismissed with a mere mention of their presence or with a
very brief description, but others are described in great
detail. The Pardoner is among these last. His description,
which is quoted in full on pages 53–54, is forty-six lines
long. He is the last of all the pilgrims to be described, and
he is placed in this position of emphasis as one of a pair. He
and the Summoner, who is described at exactly equal length
immediately before him, are presented as boon companions, riding together and singing in unison 'Com hider,
love, to me' (*GP* 674). This distinctly worldly song might
seem inappropriate for two officers of the Church, but it
expresses accurately the nature of their devotion. Their

hearts are in the world, and above all in the profit they can make for themselves out of their ecclesiastical function. This indeed is what we have come to expect of Chaucer's presentation of the Church: of the eight descriptions of ecclesiastical figures in *The General Prologue*, only one, that of the Parson, is unequivocally favourable, and that, in its generality and its reliance on denials of corruption ('He was a shepherde and *noght* a mercenarie' (*GP* 516)), seems to depict an ideal opposed to experience. The Summoner and the Pardoner are given far more detailed physical descriptions, the one red-faced and covered with hideous spots ('Of his visage children were aferd' (*GP* 630)), and the other smooth-chinned, dressed in a ghastly parody of fashion, but with eyes staring like a hare's. Together they make a horrifying pair, whose repellent outward appearance fully expresses their inner corruption. They have completely betrayed the trust placed in them by a Church which, in using them, is itself a traitor to its own ideals.

## Pardoners in the medieval Church

The function of a pardoner in the medieval Church will require some explanation. Punishments were imposed on members of the Church for their sins, and these 'penances' might take various forms, such as repeating prayers or psalms, fasting, or other forms of self-mortification. Gradually the practice grew up of allowing sinners to exchange one form of punishment for another, and particularly of allowing them to contribute alms instead of performing a physical penance. By the fourteenth century the theory known as the Treasury of Grace had developed. According to this, the Church was the guardian of the merits of Christ, the Virgin, and the saints. Their merits were more than enough to compensate for all the sins that mankind might commit, and so it was possible for the Church, as keeper of the Treasury, to distribute them among its members. Thus individual penance came to seem unnecessary: all that was needed was true penitence and payment in money or goods. Thus the sinner would be dispensed from his penance, and the Church would obtain resources for carrying out good works.

Special officers were required for carrying out such exchanges: they were called *quaestores* in Latin, pardoners in English. They might be priests or monks, but they might also, like Chaucer's Pardoner, be laymen employed as professionals. Their work would be carefully regulated by the higher authorities of the Church; they would require written authorization, signed and sealed by a bishop or by the pope himself; they would be allowed to remit the punishments only of those who were truly penitent, and their gains would have to be handed over to their superiors. This is what pardoners had originally been; but if we turn from this summary to the pardoner Chaucer describes, we find not a replica but an appalling parody.

Certain elements remain. A *quaestor* needed an episcopal licence, and Chaucer's Pardoner has not just one but several, with the seals of all possible authorities dangling from them:

> First I pronounce whennes that I come,
> And thanne my bulles shewe I, alle and some.
> Oure lige lordes seel on my patente,
> That shewe I first, my body to warente,
> That no man be so boold, ne preest ne clerk,
> Me to destourbe of Cristes hooly werk.
> And after that thanne telle I forth my tales.
> Bulles of popes and of cardinales,
> Of patriarkes and bishopes I shewe. (49–57)

He might possibly have had a genuine licence from 'oure lige lord', the local bishop, but only the very simple could expect him to be authorized as well by 'popes', 'cardinales', 'patriarkes' and 'bishopes'. These other documents must surely be fakes, intended to dazzle the impressionable. The Pardoner is careful to point out that he can offer no help to those who have on their consciences sins so appalling that they have not dared to confess them:

> Goode men and wommen, o thing warne I yow:
> If any wight be in this chirche now
> That hath doon sinne horrible, that he
> Dar nat for shame of it yshriven be,
> Or any womman, be she yong or old,
> That hath ymaad hir housbonde cokewold,
> Swich folk shal have no power ne no grace
> To offren to my relikes in this place.
> And whoso findeth him out of swich blame,
> He wol come up and offre in Goddes name,
> And I assoille him by the auctoritee
> Which that by bulle ygraunted was to me. (91–102)

But this apparent scrupulosity is really a lever for his own advantage, for naturally none of his audience will wish to admit publicly that his or her conscience is burdened in this way. Instead, they will all come rushing forward with their offerings simply to prove that they are not in mortal sin. Moreover, though the Pardoner reminds his audience that they must have confessed their 'sinne horrible' before he will release them from their penance, he goes on to claim that he will then *assoille* (absolve) them. He makes the claim more explicit at the end of his Tale, when he turns to his audience in order to exploit the story's effect on their emotions:

> Now, goode men, God foryeve yow youre trespas,
> And ware yow fro the sinne of avarice!
> Myn hooly pardoun may yow alle warice,

8

So that ye offre nobles or sterlinges,
Or elles silver broches, spoones, ringes.
Boweth youre heed under this hooly bulle!
Cometh up, ye wives, offreth of youre wolle!
Youre names I entre heer in my rolle anon;
Into the blisse of hevene shul ye gon.
I yow assoille by myn heigh power,
Yow that wol offre, as clene and eek as cleer
As ye were born.                                              (618–29)

Looke which a seuretee is it to yow alle
That I am in youre felaweshipe yfalle,
That may assoille yow, bothe moore and lasse,
Whan that the soule shal fro the body passe.        (651–4)

Clearly he is claiming the power to absolve sinners not only
from the penance for their sins (*a poena*) but also from the
sins themselves (*a culpa*). He is offering to *warice* (cure)
them of the effect of sin, to restore them to the innocence of
a newly born child, to send them straight to heaven at the
moment of death; but these powers belonged only to a
priest, not to a lay *quaestor*. The Pardoner's constant trick
is to usurp the role of a priest, and to exploit it for
histrionic purposes—it is the role itself that he finds
attractive and profitable, not the responsibilities that
should go with it.

I stonde lyk a clerk in my pulpet,                    (105)

he says; and preaching is another of the priest's powers that
he lays claim to. His whole offering to the pilgrims is in the
form of a specimen sermon, with the Tale itself as an
illustration of his text; but lay *quaestores* were in general
specifically prohibited from preaching.

With the role of priest he combines that of medicine-man
or witch-doctor. The trappings he makes most play with

are spurious holy relics, with the power (as he says) to work miracles. Among those mentioned in *The General Prologue* are the veil of the Blessed Virgin (actually a pillow-case) and a piece of the sail from St Peter's boat. Later we hear of the transparent cases

Ycrammed ful of cloutes and of bones,    (62)

which will heal and protect men and beasts, and even cure jealousy; of a mitten which will ensure a good crop to anyone who has put his hand in it; and of other relics, of unspecified power, available for kissing by the faithful if a suitable offering is made. All this is little different from a claim to magical powers, and though it does not take in Harry Bailly, the Host, it is evidently effective among the Pardoner's usual audiences, for he claims to make a hundred marks a year by his 'craft'. Here a last difference from the *quaestor* as he should be emerges. The true *quaestor* collects money for the Church, but the Pardoner keeps all he gains for his own profit, and indeed boasts of the fact. The constant theme of his preaching is

ware yow fro the sinne of avarice!    (619)

but avarice is his own ruling passion. He is aware of the paradox, and calls it constantly to our attention.

### Evidence about fourteenth-century pardoners

How are we to explain this vast difference between the *quaestor* according to the canons of the Church and Chaucer's Pardoner? We may feel tempted to suppose that Chaucer was simply inventing an anti-ecclesiastical satire to shock his audience and make them laugh. But historical evidence shows that in the Pardoner he has drawn an accurate picture of the *quaestor* as he really was in the fourteenth century. The original idea of the office had become utterly corrupted, and historical warrant can be found for every aspect of the corruption that Chaucer depicts.

In 1390 Pope Boniface IX issued a letter in which he exposed some of the very abuses presented by Chaucer. There are false pardoners, he says, who 'affirm that they are sent by us or by the legates or nuncios of the apostolic see, and that they have been given a mission . . . to receive money for us and the Roman Church, and they go about the country under these pretexts'. Chaucer's Pardoner similarly claims to come from Rome, and the pilgrim Chaucer of *The General Prologue* reports his claim unquestioningly:

> With him ther rood a gentil PARDONER
> Of Rouncivale, his freend and his compeer,
> That streight was comen fro the court of Rome.
> (GP 671–3)

> His walet lay biforn him in his lappe,
> Bretful of pardoun, comen from Rome al hoot.
> (GP 688–9)

The Pardoner is presented not only as having come from Rome, but as being 'of Rouncivale'—that is to say, as being employed to collect alms by the Chapel and Hospital of Our Lady of Rouncivalle at Charing Cross, just outside London. He could really have held this position, but there are grounds for suspicion, because in the 1380s warrants were issued to arrest persons claiming to be collecting alms for the Rouncivalle Hospital but converting their receipts to their own use. Once again Chaucer is following historical fact. Boniface adds that these false *quaestores* 'proclaim to the faithful and simple people the real or pretended authorizations which they have received; and, irreverently abusing those which are real, in pursuit of infamous and hateful gain, they carry further their impudence by mendaciously attributing to themselves false and pretended authorizations of this kind'. We have just seen how Chaucer's Pardoner displays his many 'bulles' in this way; and Chaucer follows Pope Boniface in leaving us in doubt as to whether they were 'real or pretended authorizations'. Boniface was right in thinking forgery likely; in 1378 a certain 'Thomas Pardoner' was arrested as a 'forger of the seal of the Lord the Pope'.

Chaucer's Pardoner offers absolution *a poena et a culpa*; and there are documents to show that in this too he was only following the practice of the time. In 1340 the bishop of Durham issued a warning against pretended *quaestores* who 'absolve the perjured, homicides, usurers, and other sinners who confess to them; and, on receipt of a little money, grant remission for ill-atoned crimes'. In 1369 Pope Urban V wrote to the archbishop of Canterbury, also complaining of *quaestores* in England who sold absolution *a poena et a culpa*. The Pardoner's preaching activities are fully paralleled in fourteenth-century documents; indeed, Pope Urban spoke of *quaestores* who usurped the pulpit from the parish priest, prevented him from celebrating mass, and collected the offerings themselves. It was perhaps in this way that the Pardoner

> whan that he fond
> A povre person dwellinge upon lond,
> Upon a day he gat him moore moneye
> Than that the person gat in monthes tweye.   (*GP* 703–6)

The use of relics as miracle-working and profit-producing devices was extremely common in the Middle Ages. Chaucer seems hardly to have exaggerated at all in describing his

Pardoner's monstrous deceptions. St Peter's sail and Our Lady's veil are no more improbable—perhaps less— than St Peter's vest (for which King Edward III in 1363 had paid 100 shillings) and some of Our Lady's milk (which was shown to pilgrims at Walsingham). Such practices are part of the materialism (as we might now call it) that characterized late-medieval religious orthodoxy and that forms an important context for *The Pardoner's Tale*. Religion had become materialistic in two senses. First, it was deeply integrated into and compromised by the economic fabric of medieval society; sin was a form of debt owed to God, that could be repaid by material means including the building or decoration of churches and the purchase of masses or of indulgences such as pardoners had to offer. Second, spiritual power was seen as not just symbolized by but inherent in material objects, at every level from the comfortingly or terrifyingly real presence of Christ's body in the Eucharistic bread down to the potency attributed to the bones and garments of saints. Only by the mutilation of material bodies—the tearing of Christ on the Cross, the division of his body in the Eucharist, the martyrdom of saints—could spiritual power be released; and bones and garments formed the goal of the Canterbury pilgrimage itself, at the shrine of St Thomas à Becket. When Harry Bailly coarsely rejects the Pardoner's offer to let him be the first to kiss his relics, exclaiming:

> Thou woldest make me kisse thyn olde breech,
> And swere it were a relik of a seint,
> Though it were with thy fundement depeint! (662–4)

medieval readers would recall that among the relics available for kissing at Canterbury were the hair breeches worn by St Thomas next to his skin as a form of self-mortification—an object at once holy and disgusting. This is the kind of power the Pardoner aims to exploit for his own profit; but in Chaucer's time the beliefs and practices associated with this material spirituality were being questioned by the Oxford theologian John Wyclif and his followers, the Lollards. Lollardy has been described as a 'premature Reformation',[1] and *The Pardoner's Tale* could be read as an early exploration of the conflicting forces that were to make the sixteenth-century Reformation inevitable. Chaucer had Lollard friends and may have had some sympathy with Lollard attitudes if not with Wyclif's heterodox theological teachings. In *The Pardoner's Tale*, spiritual concepts are systematically degraded by being transmuted into material forms—the Treasury of Grace into the *tresor* of florins, Mary's motherhood into that of our 'Leeve mooder' (445) the earth. The Tale derives much of its disturbing power from a tension between intense belief in the spiritual value of the material and the bodily, and a correspondingly intense and contemptuous scepticism.

## *The poetic effect of Chaucer's Pardoner*

It seems, then, that, grotesquely exaggerated as Chaucer's Pardoner may appear, his way of life is that of a possible, if not typical, *quaestor* of the fourteenth century. But to defend Chaucer against the charge of distorting historical truth is not to say very much about his *poetic* achievement in *The Pardoner's Prologue and Tale*. Chaucer was by no means the only writer of his time to present a pardoner unfavourably. William Langland had emphasized in *Piers*

---

[1] Anne Hudson, *The Premature Reformation: Wycliffite Texts and Lollard History* (Clarendon Press, 1988).

*Plowman* (a poem written in London and probably known to Chaucer) the difference between God's pardon and the 'pardon' that is simply a matter of words, and had given a satirical description of a *quaestor* which follows exactly the same lines as Chaucer's:

> There prechide a pardoner as he a prest were;
> Broughte forth a bulle with bisshopis selis
> And seide that hymself mighte assoile hem alle
> Of falsnesse of fastyng and of avowes broken.
> Lewide men levide hym wel and likide his speche;
> Comen up knelynge to kissen his bulle.
> He bunchede hem with his brevet and bleride here eiyen
> And raughte with his rageman ryngis and brochis.[1]

A pardoner preached there as if he were a priest; he brought out a licence with bishops' seals on it, and said that he had power to absolve them all for breaking fasts or vows. Ignorant men believed him and liked what he said; they came forward on their knees to kiss his licence. He thrust his letter of indulgence in their faces and bleared their eyes and with his charter seized rings and brooches.

This offers the same evidence as Chaucer, even down to the 'ryngis and brochis' that are accepted instead of money. But Langland's stern and laconic analysis has a quite different effect from Chaucer's treatment of the same material, and it is this effect with which we must now concern ourselves, if we wish to understand what Chaucer has to offer us that cannot be found in pontifical or archiepiscopal letters or anywhere else at all.

The effect the Pardoner has on us, as Chaucer describes him in *The General Prologue*, is at once comic, contempt-ible, and sinister. The comedy is not purely satirical; it does not preclude enjoyment in its object, and in this it is very typical of Chaucer. Through him, we can delight in the

[1] *Piers Plowman: The A Version*, ed. George Kane (Athlone Press, 1960), Prologue, 65–72.

roguery of a thoroughgoing rogue, and so we can take pleasure in the details of the Pardoner's trickery—the pillow-case which is supposed to be Our Lady's veil, the 'pigges bones' which serve for holy relics, and the special skill he puts into singing an 'offertorie'.

But through this pleasure runs a strong vein of contempt, which surfaces not so much in his actions as in his physical appearance. He rides along as a ghastly parody of a fashionable young man, with his hood left off 'for jolitee' and his yellow hair spread out over his shoulders. 'Him thoughte he rood al of the newe jet' (*GP* 684)—he rode along in the very latest fashion (in his own opinion). He is a parody not just of fashion but of 'normal' manhood:

> A voys he hadde as smal as hath a goot.
> No berd hadde he, ne nevere sholde have;
> As smothe it was as it were late shave.
> I trowe he were a gelding or a mare.    (*GP* 690–3)

Despite its farmyard bluntness, the exact significance of the last line is elusive—it makes no definitive statement but means something like: 'I suppose he must have been castrated or female.' This indefiniteness has not discouraged scholars from attempting to give it an exact interpretation. The Pardoner has been seen as a eunuch, and his eunuchry understood as symbolizing spiritual sterility or heresy or inner despair, or as driving him to use 'his verbal arts, documents, relics as substitutes [for his missing virility] . . . in the belief that they can make him whole'. He has also been interpreted as a homosexual, perhaps engaged in an 'unnatural' relationship with the Summoner, his companion in *The General Prologue*; and in recent years his supposed homosexuality has been associated with 'anguished self-division' or 'spiritual torment', with 'the position of the victim', and with a tragically frustrated longing for love and fellowship. One critic goes so far as to state that 'The goal of the final scene, as of all the Pardoner's maneuvers, is a kiss ... expressing genuine acceptance of his humanity.'[1] It is understandable that Chaucer's elusiveness should incite his readers to fill the resulting gaps with their own fantasies, but it is important to grasp that no such interpretations can be regarded as certain, and that many of those mentioned (only a small selection from recent discussion) are historically improbable. As one scholar has pointed out:

> Medieval people do not ... seem to have defined them-selves by sexual orientation ... To medieval theologians, lawyers and devotional writers, there were different kinds of sexual acts—between people of different sexes, between people of the same sex, between people and animals—and all had some kind of taint attached. But there was no clear notion of being one or the other kind of sexual being.[2]

Moreover, even if Chaucer had possessed a modern conception of homosexuality and had attributed it to the Pardoner, there is little reason to suppose that he would have viewed it with modern understanding or sympathy. His Pardoner, not unlike Shakespearean villains such as Richard III and Iago, hovers disturbingly between the

---

[1] For some of these views, see Robert P. Miller, 'Chaucer's Pardoner, the Scriptural Eunuch, and the *Pardoner's Tale*', *Speculum*, 30 (1955); W. C. Curry, *Chaucer and the Mediaeval Sciences*, 2nd edn (Allen and Unwin, 1960); Monica E. McAlpine, 'The Pardoner's Homosexuality and How it Matters', *Publications of the Modern Language Association of America*, 95 (1980); Carolyn Dinshaw, *Chaucer's Sexual Poetics* (University of Wisconsin Press, 1989); Lee Patterson, *Chaucer and the Subject of History* (University of Wisconsin Press, 1991).

[2] Caroline Walker Bynum, *Fragmentation and Redemption: Essays on Gender and the Human Body in Medieval Religion* (Zone Books, 1992), pp.85–6.

comic and sinister. Behind these effects no inner self is revealed save what *we* may choose to supply; and indeed it might be argued that precisely this absence of inwardness, of any self-awareness beyond the will to power and the satisfaction of desire, would be a necessary condition of the way of life Chaucer imagines for him. As with Iago, there is something so frightening about the Pardoner's inner emptiness that we may find it hard to accept.

## THE PARDONER'S PROLOGUE

After being described in *The General Prologue*, the Pardoner makes one or two interjections while the Wife of Bath is speaking, but his main contribution to the pilgrimage comes after *The Physician's Tale*. The Physician has told an austere story of sin and retribution, concerning a wicked magistrate's attempt to misuse the law in order to seduce the beautiful and virtuous daughter of a knight. He is prevented only by her father's killing her to save her from the magistrate's power, and the magistrate in turn is cast into prison and commits suicide. The Host is much affected by this story. His feelings, whether sympathetic or contemptuous, are aroused as readily by fiction as by reality; and, after lamenting and moralizing over this sad story for a while, he declares that he needs some remedy for his grief—either one provided by the Physician himself, or something to drink, or a more cheerful story. He therefore calls on the Pardoner to 'Telle us som mirthe or japes right anon' (33). The Pardoner agrees without hesitation, only saying that he must first stop at an inn the pilgrims are just passing, in order to have a drink and a snack. But at this the 'gentils' among the pilgrims—those of higher social rank and hence of more refined tastes (such as, presumably, the Knight and the Prioress)—hastily cry out that the Pardoner must not tell them 'ribaudye' but 'som moral thing'. It is obvious from the Pardoner's appearance and behaviour that he is a rogue, who might be expected to tell a grossly indecent story; and, since he is proposing to take a drink first, the 'gentils' have reason to be worried at the thought of what impropriety he might produce once drunk. Perhaps surprisingly, he agrees at once to the demand of the 'gentils', but still says that he must pause and drink while he is thinking of 'som honest thing'.

At this stage we may imagine the pilgrims gathered in the tavern to listen to what the Pardoner has to say, though at what point, if any, the journey towards Canterbury is resumed is not clear. Some readers of *The Pardoner's Tale* have been convinced that the whole narrative is delivered in the tavern, and since the Tale itself is about three drunken revellers, there would be a certain appropriateness in that. But since Chaucer provides no indication of the setting whatever, and does not even indicate whether the pilgrims are riding or resting, it can hardly be of much importance. We may visualize it as we choose. Instead of starting straight away on his 'honest' Tale, the Pardoner begins reminiscing about his own technique as a preacher. Reminiscence passes imperceptibly into demonstration, and back into reminiscence; he harangues the pilgrims as if they were his congregation, and then explains that he was only acting a part. Lastly, in detail and with vigour, he expounds his own motives in his preaching: partly malice, but fundamentally avarice. Now much of the detail the Pardoner supplies about his techniques is, as we have seen, historically accurate. The display first of impressively sealed documents and then of rags and bones which he calls relics; the monstrous claims he makes for the miraculous powers of these relics; the assertion that he has authority to absolve all who make offerings to them: all this matches the historical and literary record.

But at first sight it may be difficult to explain in realistic terms his exposure of his own motives. He admits that his technique is a *gaude* (trick), a matter of *false japes* (deceiving lies), intended solely to make his audience free in giving him money. With devastating bluntness, he remarks that

> myn entente is nat but for to winne,
> And nothing for correccioun of sinne.
> I rekke nevere, whan that they been beried,
> Though that hir soules goon a-blakeberied. (117–20)

He repeats the same assertion of motive, and himself points out the paradox that he satisfies his own avarice by preaching against the avarice of others:

> But shortly myn entente I wol devise:
> I preche of no thing but for coveitise.
> Therfore my theme is yet, and evere was,
> *Radix malorum est Cupiditas*.
> Thus kan I preche again that same vice
> Which that I use, and that is avarice. (137–42)

He ends his prologue with a confident elaboration of his intentions, the blatant assertion of a will directed towards material success:

> What, trowe ye that whiles I may preche,
> And winne gold and silver for I teche,
> That I wol live in poverte wilfully?
> Nay, nay, I thoghte it nevere, trewely!
> For I wol preche and begge in sondry landes;
> I wol nat do no labour with mine handes,
> Ne make baskettes, and live therby,

> By cause I wol nat beggen idelly.
> I wol noon of the apostles countrefete;
> I wol have moneie, wolle, chese, and whete,
> Al were it yeven of the povereste page,
> Or of the povereste widwe in a village,
> Al sholde hir children sterve for famine.
> Nay, I wol drinke licour of the vine,
> And have a joly wenche in every toun.    (153–67)

In this passage the assertion of will is enacted in the seven-times repeated 'I wol' and in the scathing annihilation of the conventional prejudices the Pardoner attributes to his listeners: 'What, trowe ye . . .? . . . Nay, nay . . .'. The will's object is present in the unashamedly specific 'moneie, wolle, chese, and whete' and 'joly wenches'. The last may well be an idle boast; but that is beside the point.

### *Realism and convention in the Pardoner's confession*

But why does the Pardoner disclose his aims and intentions in this way? Surely it would pay him to keep quiet about his villainy, and allow himself to appear as a preacher whose purpose is to save souls, not line his purse? His boasting about his avarice seems to undermine his means of satisfying it. Such an objection is based partly on a misunderstanding of Chaucer's art. On the surface it is often realistic, so realistic that it may deceive us into supposing that what it offers is actual reality, a slice of life itself. But Chaucer's realism of detail is usually only a technique, employed to supply insights and pleasures that total realism cannot achieve. *The Wife of Bath's Prologue* is an outstanding example. The Wife, by way of introduction to her Tale, tells us the whole story of her married life and the philosophy of sex and marriage she has deduced from her varied experience. (She has had no fewer than five husbands, and has fought with all of them.) As she speaks we sometimes seem to hear the very voice of a vigorous uneducated woman, mesmerized in her reminiscences by the concrete detail of experience, and losing her way among digressions just as any real person might:

> But now, sire, lat me se, what shal I seyn?
> A ha! by God, I have my tale ageyn.

But if we look below this realistic surface, we find that the material of her Prologue, anecdotal and moralizing, is drawn from a whole collection of learned sources in Latin and French, by authors as various as Theophrastus, St Jerome, Walter Map and Eustache Deschamps, whom it is most unlikely that a 'real' Wife of Bath could have read. In this way, Chaucer can simultaneously evoke the vigorous sexuality and appetite for experience that are expressed in the Wife's realism of speech, and provide argument on the question of marriage itself far more searching than anything an actual Wife of Bath would have thought of. There is a disparity between the spontaneous surface and the learned core, but surface and core co-operate to achieve a more powerful effect than either could gain separately. A parallel may be found in the late-medieval visual arts. There, too, realism of detail is frequently combined with stylization of structure. In a famous *Pietà* by Rogier van der Weyden, for example, the detailed surface of things is minutely realistic—the texture of cloth and the folds it falls in, or the horrifyingly lifelike wounds on Christ's body—and yet the body as a whole is depicted quite unrealistically in both posture and proportions, in a way that expresses the pathos and anguish of the event far more vividly than realism could do.

Similarly in *The Pardoner's Prologue*. On the surface lie

details so accurate that we can verify them from historical sources. But beneath them we find an 'unrealistic' literary convention, that of the confession. In real life people do not usually expound their own bad motives with the freedom that the Pardoner uses. Chaucer might allow these motives to appear gradually and surreptitiously from beneath a hypocritical front, but that strategy would be effective only in a much longer narrative such as a novel. In a short, concentrated work such as *The Pardoner's Prologue and Tale*, the Pardoner's true motives can best be revealed directly by himself in a confession to all who care to listen. Such confessions are extremely common in earlier medieval literature, and the Pardoner's is closely related to the confession of Faux-Semblant (False Seeming) in the *Roman de la Rose*, a thirteenth-century French poem which Chaucer had translated at an early stage of his literary career. There the speaker of the confession is a personification, who is not supposed to possess any inner life, and it is delivered not voluntarily but under orders from the God of Love. It is called a sermon, and it expounds Faux-Semblant's way of life, which flourishes especially among friars: concealed by religious robes, he claims the power, granted by papal authority—'For of the Pope I have the bulle'—to confess and absolve the laity, competing with the parish priests who ought to receive their confessions. Thus he gains money for himself—

> But I wole have the fatte sheep;
> Lat parish prestes have the lene!

—and his aim, like the Pardoner's, is to satisfy his appetite: 'I wole fillen . . . / My paunche of good mete and wyn.' In short, he explains, 'To wynnen is alwey myn entente.' Chaucer's debt to this confession is obvious: the Pardoner is Faux-Semblant translated from begging friar to the lower and more squalid level of *quaestor*; he shares with his predecessor a cynical lack of concern for the souls of those to whom he purports to offer salvation, and above all he shares the association of pardon with profit.

In Faux-Semblant's case confession is simply a literary convention, and therefore the discrepancy between self-concealment and self-revelation needs no explaining in terms of motive. The case of the Pardoner is more complicated. For one thing, it includes a stronger emphasis on confession itself and thus on the parallel between his own confession and the confessions he elicits from his victims as the condition of granting them pardon. For another, the Pardoner's confession has been given a realistic ground in the pause to take a drink—if he is not exactly drunk, his tongue has at least been loosened by 'a draughte of corny ale'. Again, he is not facing his usual congregation of 'lewed peple', but a temporary audience of pilgrims to whom he is giving a demonstration and perhaps feels that he can afford to expose himself. But there is a more fundamental consideration than these. The fact is that a great deal of the poem's force is directly derived *from* the confessional element itself, not achieved *in spite of* that element. If we read *The Pardoner's Prologue* responsively, giving ourselves up to Chaucer's imaginative world without troubling about probability, there is no question of simply *accepting* a convention: we are carried away by the force of the speaker's self-exposure. In that self-exposure lies his power over all his audiences—his congregations, the pilgrims, and ourselves. An essential feature of the evil embodied in the Pardoner is that it should be self-confident, blatant, the very opposite of ashamed of itself. The Pardoner does not simply 'confess' his wickedness, but thrusts it upon the pilgrims, and re-enacts it with the irresistible power of an actor—an actor, as it were, playing himself, fashioning a self out of words by sheer will-power. This self-dramatization is the secret of his success as a preacher: it is a triumph of the will projecting itself outwards in threat, denunciation, or seductive whisper, and absorbing its audience's will, as well as their money, into itself. The Pardoner glories in the power he possesses, and characterizes it metaphorically in the repeated image of a poisonous snake. Instead of the 'dowve sitting on a berne' (111), symbol of the Holy Spirit by whom the Christian preacher should be inspired, he becomes a venomous serpent, symbol of the Devil:

Thanne wol I stinge him with my tonge smerte ...     (127)

Thus spitte I out my venym under hewe
Of hoolinesse ...     (135–6)

This image draws its power not only from common experience but from Scriptural tradition: the Psalmist says of his enemies: 'They have sharpened their tongues like a serpent; the venom of asps is under their lips' (Psalm 139:3).[1] The snake, moreover, is supposed to hypnotize its victims by staring at them. Similarly, the Pardoner, at least when dealing with the pilgrims, fixes them with his 'glaringe eyen' and draws them into his own evil. This evil arouses horror, certainly, but it also arouses fascination, and a fascination which has nothing to do with sympathy. One scholar has written that the Pardoner 'is to be pitied

[1] Biblical quotations are from the Douai translation of the medieval Latin Bible.

rather than censured',[1] but surely pity and censure are both lost in this strange fusion of fascination and horror.

## *The art of preaching*

The Pardoner, then, is irresistibly self-assertive. But he presents himself in the role of a preacher, and self-assertive is exactly what a preacher ought not to be. In the Middle Ages the sermon was one of the most important literary forms, and much thought was given to its construction. This thought was embodied in an elaborate theory of preaching, the *ars praedicandi* (art of preaching). Many works on the art of preaching (*artes praedicandi*) were written in England in the thirteenth and fourteenth centuries, and there can be little doubt that Chaucer would have been familiar with their doctrines, if only from hearing many sermons preached. Their doctrines are extremely complex, but for our purpose they may be divided into two parts, moral and technical.

According to the moral part of the medieval *ars praedicandi*, the preacher is a mouthpiece for the Holy Spirit. He is genuinely inspired, and must follow God's guidance rather than any human art. Above all, he must preach not in order to show off himself and his skill but in order to praise God and to teach and improve his neighbours. The Pardoner's aim in preaching is thus a total perversion of the *ars praedicandi* as it should be. On the other hand, he is immensely skilled in the technical part of the *ars*. He does not follow in any detail the complicated structure taught by the *artes*, but he makes virtuoso use of many of the techniques of preaching. The *theme* round which his whole sermon is elaborated is *Radix malorum est cupiditas* (St

[1] Curry, *Chaucer and the Mediaeval Sciences*, p. 70.

Paul's 1st Epistle to Timothy, 6:10: 'the desire of money is the root of all evils'), and he illustrates this *theme* with many *ensamples* (Latin *exempla*, specific incidents used to ram home a general assertion). Some of these are taken from the Bible, some from secular writers, some from everyday life; and the Tale itself is an *exemplum* told to illustrate the *theme*. The style of his sermon is made more dramatic by such appealing rhetorical figures as apostrophe—

O wombe! O bely! O stinking cod! (248)

—and onomatopoeia—'Sampsoun, Sampsoun!' (268) as an imitation of a drunkard's heavy breathing. All these devices are used frequently in the preaching section at the beginning of the Tale, cut down while the actual story is being told, and brought back with renewed force once it is ended.

The Pardoner also makes brilliant use of those spellbinding techniques that are learned from experience, rather than any formal art: the manipulation of suspense, climax, and anti-climax; the modulation from one tone of voice to another; the alternation of simplicity and complexity; and so on. His whole performance—it *is* a performance, a histrionic achievement—is extraordinarily accomplished. What is more, it works, not simply in exploiting its listeners' emotions, but in creating a genuine sense of horror at the sin it is directed against, and of terror at God's vengeance on the sinners. The Pardoner perverts the preacher's art, and yet achieves an effect even more powerful than the true preacher. He is perfectly aware of this paradox. It was indeed a commonplace of

the times, and in stating it Chaucer borrows again from the
*Roman de la Rose*:

> For certes, many a predicacioun
> Comth ofte time of yvel entencioun;
> Som for plesance of folk and flaterye,
> To be avaunced by ypocrisye,
> And som for veyne glorie, and som for hate.  (121–5)

As applied by the Pardoner, this paradox has two aspects.
One is that he preaches against avarice out of avarice and
yet genuinely succeeds in deterring people from avarice:

> Thus kan I preche again that same vice
> Which that I use, and that is avarice.
> But though myself be gilty in that sinne,
> Yet kan I maken oother folk to twynne
> From avarice, and soore to repente.  (141–5)

The other aspect is that though he is himself 'vicious', he
can still tell a 'moral tale'—a tale all the more effective
because he *is* 'vicious', and can evoke from experience the
sin he denounces:

> For though myself be a ful vicious man,
> A moral tale yet I yow telle kan,
> Which I am wont to preche for to winne.  (173–5)

This paradox, like so many aspects of the Pardoner, is
related to the religious climate of the time. Wyclif had
raised the question as to whether sacraments such as
penance and the Eucharist were valid when administered
by 'a ful vicious man'—a priest in a state of mortal sin. The
traditional view had been that, while the priest might
thereby damn himself, the sacrament would still benefit
those receiving it; Wyclif had denied this, and there is an
obvious parallel between this topical controversy and the
question of whether a tale can be morally efficacious even

though its teller is 'ful vicious'. When transferred to the sphere of literary fiction, the orthodox view may seem bewildering or horrifying rather than comforting.

## THE PARDONER'S TALE

The actual story the Pardoner tells, as has already been mentioned, is not original. A basic plot concerning two or three men who find some treasure, disregard a wise man's warning that it will cause death, and plan simultaneously to kill each other for it by poison and violence, is widely distributed throughout Europe in the Middle Ages. Like many medieval popular tales, it is probably of oriental origin, but the version closest to Chaucer's is in a sixteenth-century Italian work. This is too late to have been Chaucer's source, and in fact we do not know where Chaucer got his version of the Tale, or how much he added to it. The mysterious old man whom the revellers in *The Pardoner's Tale* meet, and who is himself seeking death, appears to be adapted from the wise man (a philosopher or hermit) who gives a warning against the treasure as a cause of death. Neither his quest for death nor that of the three revellers appears in any of the known analogues, and it seems likely that the whole theme of the quest for death was added by Chaucer. However, these questions of origin throw little light on Chaucer's own achievement in *The Pardoner's Tale*. Medieval writers, unlike modern novelists, did not normally invent their own stories. They preferred to make use of stories which already existed—often stories which had been passed on orally without the intervention of writing—and then to combine and modify these so as to adapt them to their own purposes. Chaucer, in *The Canterbury Tales*, though not in his earlier work, appears sometimes to borrow stories from oral tradition in this way, and his 'source' in such a case will naturally remain unidentifiable.

## The discourse on the sins

*The Pardoner's Tale* falls clearly into two parts. One is the actual story, and the other is a discourse on various sins (lines 197–374 in the present edition) which is inserted into the story soon after its beginning. It will be convenient to consider this discourse on the sins first; we may call it the 'sermon-interlude'. In this sermon-interlude the Pardoner displays once more the virtuosity as a preacher that we have already seen in his Prologue. He begins with a long attack on gluttony, fully illustrated with *exempla* and supported by authorities. At various points in this attack he turns to consider one special subdivision of the larger sin of gluttony, namely drunkenness, and to illustrate its unfortunate effects. By this time, he has got fully into his stride, and though he admits that he has said enough of gluttony, he turns back not to his story but to a second sin, gambling:

> Namoore of this, for it may wel suffise.
> And now that I have spoken of glotonye,
> Now wol I yow deffenden hasardrye.     (302–4)

Gambling he treats in the same way as gluttony, though more briefly, and then finally he launches an attack on a third sin, swearing. Then at last he returns to the story he had begun nearly two hundred lines earlier.

A denunciation of sins nearly two hundred lines long, inserted when the story has scarcely begun, might seem in great danger of being tedious. This danger is avoided in the sermon-interlude by the extraordinary virtuosity of technique the Pardoner displays in his preaching. The methods he adopts are astonishingly various. At one moment he is quoting sensational stories of incest and murder from the Bible; at another he is giving details of cooking procedures. Sometimes he will denounce sin from the heights, as if his voice were God's; sometimes he will speak to his listeners with the utmost familiarity and crack sly or knowing jokes as if he were nudging them in the ribs. Now he speaks bluntly and even coarsely; now he displays abstruse learning and dazzles at least the 'lewed' among the pilgrims with his scraps of theology. Variety is the essence of his art: the listeners are never allowed to rest in a single attitude of mind in case they should become bored and inattentive, and he has something for everyone.

His learning in particular demands some comment. As a preacher would be expected to do, the Pardoner bases his argument on the Bible. He quotes or alludes to a wide variety of Scriptural texts—from Genesis, Proverbs and Ecclesiasticus (relegated to the Apocrypha in Protestant Bibles), and from the Gospels and (most often of all) the epistles of St Paul. But he also quotes from at least one theological work, the *Adversus Jovinianum* of St Jerome; from this he takes the somewhat surprising idea that the eating of the apple was an example of the sin of gluttony. And he borrows also from three moralists, the first-century Stoic Seneca and the medieval Christians Pope Innocent III and John of Salisbury. None of this material is particularly recondite; it does not imply especially deep reading on Chaucer's part, but it does indicate that the sermon-interlude is not simply a flashy tissue of inaccuracies such as a real *quaestor* might have produced. It possesses a firm moral and theological foundation; and this view of it is supported by the unexpectedly close links between it and *The Parson's Tale*, the handbook on penance that concludes *The Canterbury Tales*.

*The Parson's Tale* takes the form of an analysis of the seven deadly sins and of the remedies against them, in which each sin and its various subdivisions are distinguished with minute care. In ideas, and even in wording, the sermon-interlude in *The Pardoner's Tale* and the Parson's treatise are often very similar. On gambling, to take one example, the Parson begins as follows: 'Now comth hasardrie . . ., of which comth deceite, false othes, chidinges, and alle ravynes, blaspheminge and reneying of God, and hate of his neighebores, wast of goodes, misspendinge of time, and somtime manslaughtre'. The Pardoner introduces his attack on gambling thus:

> Hasard is verray mooder of lesinges,
> And of deceite, and cursed forsweringes,
> Blaspheme of Crist, manslaughtre, and wast also
> Of catel and of time . . .                     (305–8)

The two passages are clearly similar, though the Pardoner's list is artistically abbreviated and, with a revealingly characteristic perversion, makes the order of the last three items suggest that waste of time and goods may be *more* important than manslaughter. Underlying the attractive variety of the sermon-interlude's surface can be found a theological exactness which may not be 'realistic', but which implies a theologically sensitive poet and audience.

But what is the effect of all the Pardoner's rhetoric and theology? He speaks what purports to be a prohibition of the sins of gluttony, gambling, and swearing—'Now wol I yow *deffenden* [forbid] hasardrye' (304)—and yet the effect of his preaching is not really prohibitive. By it the sins are not diminished but magnified: they come to assume gigantic proportions and a relentless activity which is given them by the vigour of Chaucer's verse and by its constant movement from one *exemplum* to another. They come to seem irresistible forces, at work wherever in time or place one turns one's glance; and, like the Pardoner himself, they arouse at the same time horror and fascination.

This ambivalent reaction is also provoked by another, related aspect of the Pardoner's treatment of the sins. As he presents them, they merge into one another. Gluttony leads to lechery, as the *exemplum* of Lot witnesses; it was also the cause of the Fall. Gambling leads to the results listed above, including lying, murder, and blasphemy, and also, as a later line insists, to other sins: 'Forswering, ire, falsnesse, homicide' (371). This last line occurs in the attack on swearing, and thus has the effect of blurring the distinction between that sin and the others. In the furnace of the Pardoner's rhetoric, all the sins are fused together into a mass more powerful and more terrifying than any single sin could be. If that mass can be given a name, it must be blasphemy. Gluttony is a form of blasphemy, as appears from St Paul's 'wombe is hir god' (line 247; compare Epistle to the Philippians 3:19). Gambling, as has been said, leads to 'cursed forsweringes' (306) and 'blaspheme of Crist' (307). And the sermon-interlude culminates in a twenty-seven-line section devoted to blasphemy itself. In this the Pardoner argues that God forbids taking his name in vain even more urgently than murder (because the prohibition of blasphemy comes earlier in the list of

Commandments). He goes on to give examples of verbal blasphemies such as medieval gamblers might use—'By Goddes precious herte' (365), 'By Goddes armes' (368), and so on. From these examples he passes directly back into the tale of the three revellers.

The process by which the sins are subsumed into a greater whole and culminate in blasphemy is relevant to the tale as well as the sermon-interlude. I have called it an interlude, and other readers have gone further and denied its relevance to the actual story. But in fact it is closely connected with the tale of the three revellers. For in them the sins are fused together as they are in the interlude: they are gluttons, gamblers, time-wasters, deceivers, murderers, and above all blasphemers. (The nature of their blasphemy will be discussed below, but the fact is clear.) It is the interlude which makes it seem natural that the theme *Radix malorum est cupiditas* should be illustrated by a tale about three blasphemous revellers; for all the sins have been merged into blasphemy in the Prologue, and their avarice is only one aspect of their general sinfulness.

## The Tale resumed

At last, then, after all this preparation, we come to the resumption of the Tale itself. Chaucer's task was to give new life and meaning to an old tale. Some of the meaning he gives it is supplied by the sermon-interlude we have just been looking at; this is his own contribution entirely, and in others of *The Canterbury Tales* too he indicates the area in which we are to look for a story's significance by inserting an apparent digression soon after the story has begun. Other meanings that he finds in the actual narrative of *The Pardoner's Tale* we shall come to in a minute. But the life he gives it, through his skill as a narrative and dramatic poet, is incomparable and unmistakable.

## The pace of the story

Especially important is Chaucer's control of the story's pace. The actual story is strikingly brief—only one-third of the whole text—and its brevity stands out all the more sharply against the expansive surrounding material. The three revellers, unmentioned previously and never named, are introduced with abrupt familiarity, as if we knew them already:

> Thise riotoures thre of whiche I telle.          (375)

The essentials of the opening scene are immediately set before us: the three revellers, already drinking at dawn, unmindful of the canonical hours, and a single sound-effect, the sinister noise of the bell being carried along in front of a corpse on its way to burial. There is no superfluous description, yet the scene is set with brilliant exactness, and the action is under way almost before we are aware of it. In what follows, brief tableaux of discussion alternate with rapid and decisive movements. The servant and the innkeeper speak of Death's power, and, with the mad rashness for which the 'first' reveller is usually spokesman—the rashness that the rapid movement of the narrative expresses—they decide to kill Death, and rush off 'al dronken in this rage' (419) to find him. There is then a pause imposed by the meeting with the deliberately-spoken old man—

> This olde man gan looke in his visage,
> And seyde thus . . .          (434–5)

—followed by a new surge of activity when he directs them to the oak tree. They run, and the rhythmic emphasis falls on the verb of motion:

> And everich of thise riotoures *ran*
> Til he cam to that tree . . .          (482–3)

Now comes another pause for discussion. The 'worst' reveller expounds his plan (or the part of it which can be told to the youngest), then the youngest is sent off to the town, and there follows the 'temptation scene'. Simultaneously with this, the youngest has thought of his plan, and he too is jerked into rapid activity. He hurries—'no lenger wolde he tarie' (565)—to the apothecary, and buys a poison which will take effect equally hurriedly:

> Ye, sterve he shal, and that in lasse while
> Than thou wolt goon a paas nat but a mile,
> This poisoun is so strong and violent.          (579–81)

Having obtained the poison, he runs (with 'ran' again emphasized as the rhyme-word) to borrow the bottles and returns to his companions. The closing events of the story—the treacherous murder and the double poisoning—are narrated without delay or artifice. 'What nedeth it to sermone of it moore?' (593), asks the Pardoner; everything happened as planned. The pace of the narrative, at first interrupted by threatening tableaux, but increasing to an almost grotesque violence, as though a film were being gradually speeded up, is expressive of the very nature of the story. It shows a kind of madness in the revellers, as, not satisfied with the inevitable approach of death, they hurl themselves towards their own death and damnation. Once the conclusion of the actual story is reached, the pace immediately slackens, and the Pardoner allows himself to expand on the simple event with a learned allusion to Avicenna and a series of rhetorical apostrophes.

## The old man

Another way in which Chaucer gives new life to an old tale is one derived from the tale itself. The basic story of the quest for death depends on our understanding the personification of death as literally true, not metaphorical, until it emerges that the revellers 'find Death' not as a person but in the shape of their own *cupiditas*.

> No lenger thanne after Deeth they soughte       (486)

comments the Pardoner when the revellers come upon the heap of gold; they need not seek for death any longer, because they have already found it. But Chaucer greatly expands the literalism of the story and in doing so once more reflects the late-medieval religious climate. He constantly makes his characters treat common metaphors as literal statements, and this gives the work a primitive, mythological quality. Death is a person to the innkeeper and the revellers as well as the boy: he is a 'privee theef' (389), a 'false traitour' (413), a dangerous enemy, who may 'do a man a dishonour' (405), but, being a person, is capable of being killed. There is literalism too in the recurrent idea (to which we shall return shortly) that the revellers' oaths by the parts of Christ's body are actually tearing that body to pieces. And the literalism of Chaucer's treatment centres in the mysterious old man whom the revellers meet.

The significance of this old man has been the subject of much controversy: he is a figure of compelling power, but it is not obvious what his status is in the poem's scheme of ideas. A common view is that he is himself Death; but surely the fact that he is seeking death, and that he points out the way to death for the revellers, makes this unlikely. They are mistaken, after all, in thinking that death is a being external to themselves: death lies within them, in the nature of their murderously egoistic desire for possessions. Other attempts to assign a meaning to the old man have ranged from identifying him with the *vetus homo* of St Paul, the 'old man, who is corrupted according to the desire of error' (Epistle to the Ephesians 4:22) and who must be cast off before one can achieve spiritual rebirth, to seeing him quite literally as an old man who directs the revellers to the tree simply to get rid of them. No such attempts have been entirely convincing, and the reason may be that, as Chaucer presents him, the old man possesses a poetic suggestiveness, an uncanny resonance, that goes beyond any possible intellectual formulation. This is what he primarily contributes to the poem.

The Tale as a whole centres in a quest for death; this quest is presented in an extended form in the actions of the three revellers, but in a different, more concentrated form it is embodied in the old man. He is seeking death not in order to destroy it but in order to die; and death evades him in a way which contrasts ironically with the way in which it lies in wait for the revellers. In him death and its approach take on a horrifyingly concrete form. If he could find someone to exchange youth for his age, he would wish to go on living; if he could die, he would; but instead he is condemned to a permanent old age. His face is 'ful pale and welked' (452), and he refers to the wasting away of his 'flessh and blood and skin' (446) as if it were a process occurring visibly before the revellers' eyes. In his state of bodily dissolution, he is like a living version of one of the figures on late-medieval tombs that show the deceased person as a decaying corpse. In medieval lyrics on death, an old man frequently figures as 'a herald and warning of the grave';[1] the old man of *The Pardoner's Tale*, by contrast, is a warning of the gruesome outcome if the revellers were to achieve their goal, so that human beings aged but never died. The earth is commonly said to be our mother; he treats this metaphor as literally true, and knocks continually on the earth with his stick, saying, 'Leeve mooder, leet me in!' (445). Chaucer borrowed from a Latin elegy by Maximian that he had probably studied at school the idea of an old man knocking on the ground and begging it to receive him, but he added the sinister notion that the knocking is the constant tap of the old man's stick as he walks about. It has been suggested that this quest to re-enter the mother may be an image of spiritual rebirth, deriving from Nicodemus's question to Jesus, 'How can a man be born when he is old? Can he enter a second time into his mother's womb and be born again?' (John 3:4).[2] Yet the old man's very literalism implies that confusion of the spiritual with the material which characterizes late-medieval Christianity and is found throughout the Tale. Nicodemus himself is involved in this confusion, and Jesus has to explain to him that 'That which is born of the flesh is flesh: and that which is born of the Spirit is spirit' (3:6). In *The Pardoner's Tale* both life and death are horribly fleshly, and the old man's desire to re-enter his mother

[1] Rosemary Woolf, *The English Religious Lyric in the Middle Ages* (Clarendon Press, 1968), p.102.
[2] Derek Pearsall, *The Canterbury Tales* (Allen and Unwin, 1985), p.104.

evokes not spiritual regeneration but the forbidden Oedipal act of incest. The old man expresses his wish to die in another vividly concrete form, and one which reminds us of the vanity of earthly life: he wishes he could exchange his chestful of clothes for the 'heyre clowt' (450) in which a dead man is wrapped in his coffin. In this figure, on the brink of death, yet not dead, the wretched subjection of human existence to death is conveyed more powerfully than it could be by straightforward theological assertion. The revellers delight in their life in this world, and yet this is what it amounts to: a state of being in which death itself must be begged for. The old man is a figure at once inescapably concrete and uncannily suggestive: he produces a shiver of apprehension, a physiological response which can never be fully resolved into a statement of 'meaning'. The effect is unusual in Chaucer, who creates complexity more often than mystery. The old man has more in common with the Green Knight in the famous romance *Sir Gawain and the Green Knight*, by an anonymous contemporary of Chaucer's: his power derives precisely from the way that he defeats all attempts at definition.

### Blasphemy in the Tale

The old man, then, is used by Chaucer to open a door into a new dimension of his Tale—a door through which blows the cold air of mortality. If Chaucer had not added him to the story of the three revellers, its significance would be greatly lessened. But there is another level of significance in *The Pardoner's Tale* which is implicit in the story itself, and which Chaucer has brought into the open with many small touches. This is perhaps its deepest significance of all. The

Pardoner, we have seen, is a blasphemer: his very way of life is a blasphemous parody of the divine values it ought properly to serve. We have also seen how he interrupts his Tale with a homiletic interlude culminating in an attack on blasphemy. The Tale is about blasphemers: not only are the revellers' other sins forms of blasphemy, but they persistently commit verbal assaults on Christ's body. We are told of these as the story opens:

> Hir othes been so grete and so dampnable
> That it is grisly for to heere hem swere.
> Oure blissed Lordes body they totere—
> Hem thoughte that Jewes rente him noght ynough.   (186–9)

After the sermon-interlude we hear examples of how the revellers tear Christ's body to pieces, and they are of the same type as those mentioned under blasphemy in the interlude: 'Ye, Goddes armes' (406), 'I make avow to Goddes digne bones' (409), 'By Goddes dignitee' (415). Oaths such as these echo throughout the Tale, and they have two effects. First, echoing those 'Devotional pictures of Christ's wounds [which] underlined the horror of the Crucifixion by representing Christ himself as fragmented by our sins',[1] they are the most striking form of a pervasive feature of the Pardoner's performance—an obsession with the mutilation of bodies. It was noted above that for late-medieval Christianity bodily mutilation was the means of releasing spiritual power; but here bones and bodily parts seem to be obsessively imagined for their own sake, almost as in a horror movie. There are the Pardoner's relics, 'scraps and chips of saints',[2] whether real or fake; the 'harde bones' from which cooks knock out the marrow

[1] Bynum, *Fragmentation and Redemption*, p.280.
[2] Dinshaw, *Chaucer's Sexual Poetics*, p.164.

(255–6) for the sake of gluttons who are themselves imagined as separate bodily parts, 'the shorte throte, the tendre mouth' (231), the gross belly 'Fulfilled of dong and of corrupcioun', and the foul 'ende' (249–50); the 'bicched bones two' (370) that are the dice used by gamblers; the 'flessh and blood and skin' (446) that form the old man's disintegrating body; the Pardoner's 'handes and . . . tonge' (112) working with autonomous energy as he preaches; and the many parts of Christ's body mentioned in the revellers' repeated oaths. If the Pardoner is really a *gelding*, then his body too is mutilated; and at the Tale's end, after he has warned that the bodies of the pilgrims may be broken apart—

> Paraventure ther may fallen oon or two
> Doun of his hors, and breke his nekke atwo        (649–50)

—the Host threatens to mutilate *him*, turning his *coillons* into one of his own relics. The intensely carnal and incarnational focus of late-medieval religion is transformed in *The Pardoner's Tale* into a surrealistic fantasy in which body-parts have taken over the world.

The second effect of the repeated oaths is that they serve to create an irony by which the revellers come under a divine judgement that they themselves invoke. A particularly striking example of how God's name is thus taken in vain, and yet not in vain, occurs when the youngest reveller is alone, and

> 'O Lord!' quod he, 'if so were that I mighte
> Have al this tresor to myself allone,
> Ther is no man that liveth under the trone
> Of God that sholde live so murye as I.'        (554–7)

At that very moment he is before God's throne, the seat of judgement, and does not know it. But the oaths come most thickly earlier in the Tale, when the revellers are making their vow

> To live and dien ech of hem for oother. (417)

They swear 'many a grisly ooth' (422), and we are reminded that in doing so they tear Christ's body to pieces. Here again, once we know the story, we feel the terrifying irony by which God brings men to the ill ends they themselves desire.

The purpose of their vow, however, brings us to another kind of blasphemy: a blasphemous parody of the sacred, embodied in the very shape of the narrative. Their purpose is to bring about the death of Death: 'Deeth shal be deed, if that they may him hente' (424). But this concept of the death of Death, *mors mortis*, is a formulation traditionally used by Christian writers to express Christ's victory in the Crucifixion. It goes back to an Old Testament source, Hosea 13:14: *O mors, ero mors tua*, 'O death, I will be thy death'. The Latin text is quoted as a prophecy of the triumph of the Cross in a number of medieval literary works—Langland's *Piers Plowman* for example. Thus the revellers' purpose is presented as a profane parody of God's purpose in the Crucifixion. In this way, the Tale is especially suitable for the Pardoner to tell; nor need it surprise us that Chaucer should have thought of giving him a story which parodies something holy.

Blasphemous parody was not uncommon even in the religious literature of the Middle Ages. In a time when Christianity was unquestioned, blasphemy was perhaps more shocking than it is today, but it was also more possible (because the structure of Christianity stood too firm to be fundamentally shaken by it) and more likely (as the human reaction against an overwhelming current of reverence). In medieval religious drama, Antichrist sometimes appeared as a parody of Christ; and, even more striking, in the *Second Shepherds' Play* of the Towneley cycle the Lamb of God appears in a comic parody as a stolen sheep hidden in a cradle and disguised as the newborn child of the thief's wife. There, blasphemy co-exists with reverence and is eventually absorbed into a reverence which is the more moving and more secure against irony for including it. In *The Pardoner's Tale*, the blasphemy penetrates to the very structure of the story itself, as it has penetrated to the empty core of the Pardoner's being; and the teller and his Tale testify to the truth by reversing it, as a photographic negative 'parodies' the positive.

In the Tale, blasphemy appears elsewhere than in the quest to kill Death. The death of Death, in the sacred sense, is brought about by the sacrificial death of Christ on the Cross. However, as a result of the doctrine of the Trinity, this death can easily be represented not as a voluntary self-sacrifice by the Son, but as the sacrifice of a purely passive Son by the other members of the Trinity. Only a small shift of emphasis in this view would create a theory of the Crucifixion as a conspiracy by two members of the Trinity against the third. It appears that in the fourteenth century this shift of emphasis had occurred, and the conspiracy-theory of the Crucifixion had become a current blasphemy. It is mentioned in *Piers Plowman* in a passage regretting that those who can tell of sacred matters are not welcome at feasts. On the contrary, indeed,

Nowe is the manere at the mete, when munstrals ben stille,
The lewed ayen the lered the holy lore to dispute,
And tellen of the Trinite how two slowe the thridde.[1]

It is now the custom at meal-times, when the minstrels are
silent, for the ignorant to argue with the learned about
sacred doctrine; and, concerning the Trinity, they say that
two killed the third.

If this was a familiar idea among the *lewed* (ignorant) in the
late fourteenth century, it seems plausible to suppose that
the audience of *The Pardoner's Tale*, alerted to blasphemous parody by the 'death of Death' motif, might find a
similar parody in the part of the story in which two of a trio
of revellers plot to kill the third. The third who is sent away
and then murdered thus becomes a parody-representation
of Christ. When he returns, the others 'rive him thurgh the
sides tweye' (542), tearing his body as Christ's body was
torn on the Cross and as it is torn again by the revellers'
oaths. The blasphemous meaning is underlined by the fact
that the provisions the youngest reveller is sent to fetch are
specified as 'breed and wyn' (511)—the two elements of the
sacrament provided by Christ's torn body. Though the
story of the three revellers derives from a folk-tale,
Chaucer, by adding *The Pardoner's Prologue* and the
sermon-interlude, has given it a sufficiently theological
treatment for us to gather that his audience had some
awareness of theological issues. Not a very high degree of
theological sensitivity would be needed for the interlocking
narrative blasphemies of the Tale to become evident. They
provide a significance of the most appropriate kind.

---

[1] *Piers Plowman: An Edition of the C-Text*, ed. Derek Pearsall (Edward
Arnold, 1978), C.XI.35–7.

## THE CONCLUSION

The end of the story of the three revellers comes with their death, and this event is described by the Pardoner with a bareness, almost an offhandedness, which implies that it is the most natural thing in the world. And then, immediately, the Pardoner resumes the expansive and even inflated style that he had used in his sermon-interlude. First, he refers us to a scientific authority, the great Arab physician Avicenna, for an account of the 'signes of empoisoning' (605) displayed on the corpses of the two elder revellers—as if, for these materially minded evildoers, the damnation of the soul were represented in the distortion of the body. Then he suddenly lets fly with a thunder of *exclamationes* directed against the sins of the murderers, and reaching a climax, as usual, in blasphemy. Then, equally suddenly, the 'O' of denunciation gives way to the 'Allas' of pleading, and he asks tearfully how mankind can behave so unnaturally towards its Creator and Redeemer. With another unexpected switch, he turns from warning 'mankinde' against the sins to warning the 'goode men' who are listening to him against the 'sinne of avarice'—the whole purpose of his preaching. In persuasively jaunty rhythms he invites his congregation to make their offerings on the spot, and assures them that they will swiftly be translated from names on his list to happy souls in 'the blisse of hevene'—the very note of the insurance-salesman. Then, without warning, we are brought back to earth half-way through a line with 'And lo, sires, thus I preche' (629). It is not us or the pilgrims he is addressing, after all, but an imaginary congregation of the ignorant; we remember that his whole Tale has been only a sample of his preaching skill. If, as is likely, we have forgotten this in the excitement of the narrative, we shall be taken aback for the moment, and, while we are still reeling, the Pardoner comes up with something even more surprising:

> And lo, sires, thus I preche.
> And Jhesu Crist, that is oure soules leche,
> So graunte yow his pardoun to receive,
> For that is best; I wol yow nat deceive.　　(629–32)

The Pardoner seems to be saying that, though he may deceive his usual audiences, he will not deceive the pilgrims: to them he will admit that Christ's pardon alone, and not his, has power to save the soul. Some readers have detected in these words a depth of personal feeling that is not to be found in the rest of his patter; as though he felt a momentary repulsion against all his blasphemous falsehood—'a very paroxysm of agonized sincerity', as one scholar has put it[1]—and offered the pilgrims a last desperate glimpse of the truth against which he had blasphemed. What he says *is* the truth, of course, and in distinguishing sharply between Christ's pardon and the 'pardon' a *quaestor* offers he is stating a commonplace of medieval religious literature. But to assert that, in telling the truth, he is 'sincere' is another matter. The devil can quote Scripture to his purpose; and this 'sincerity' may be only part of a confidence-trick. With yet another unexpected change of direction, the Pardoner continues:

> But sires, o word forgat I in my tale:
> I have relikes and pardoun in my male
> As faire as any man in Engelond,
> Whiche were me yeven by the popes hond.
> If any of yow wole, of devocion,

[1] G.L. Kittredge, *Chaucer and his Poetry* (Harvard University Press, 1915), p.217.

Offren, and han myn absolucion,
Com forth anon, and kneleth heere adoun,
And mekely receiveth my pardoun.        (633–40)

He has the impudence to try the technique he has just been demonstrating on the pilgrims themselves—evidently in the hope that, while they are still under the spell of his Tale, he will have the double satisfaction of first showing them how clever he is as a swindler and then swindling them too. Perhaps it is not enough, though, to claim that he is simply insincere in his words about Christ's pardon. That may be as misleading as to claim that he is sincere. His whole method as a preacher is that of self-dramatization: he exploits his own ready emotions by making them public for the sake of gain. By working himself up he works up his audience. No doubt there are real tears in his eyes, but to speak of sincerity or insincerity is as meaningless as it would be if applied to a great actor in a play. He is neither sincere nor insincere; he is simply acting, squeezing the utmost emotion out of his own situation. His wickedness lies in having turned his own moral and spiritual life, and Christian truth itself, into a play. Has Chaucer done any better?

The Pardoner continues to direct his jaunty patter at the pilgrims. He tempts them with the thought of pardon 'Al newe and fressh' (642), like hot cakes. He reminds them, with some relish, that one or two of them may fall from their horses and break their necks on that very journey. Finally he suggests that the Host himself should set the example in making an offering and kissing the relics, 'For he is moost envoluped in sinne' (656). Will the Host be able to find a response adequate to this supreme audacity? He does not disappoint us. Like a Dr Johnson of the medieval alehouse, he sweeps the Pardoner away, utterly annihilates him, with a superb explosion of coarseness, devoted mainly to the Pardoner's lack of sexual capacity. It does its work so effectively that the Pardoner is reduced to silence—he who made such a good living by his tongue, and who managed to interrupt even the incessantly loquacious Wife of Bath. The Host seems scarcely aware of his own power in invective: he is puzzled and hurt at the Pardoner's failure to reply, and says he will not play with anyone so quick to lose his temper. Everyone laughs; but the Knight, always tactful, and conscious of his responsibilities as the pilgrim of highest secular rank, speaks politely to both, and persuades them to kiss and make up. With that unlikely embrace the Tale ends and the pilgrims ride on.

In the conclusion of *The Pardoner's Tale* Chaucer has displayed one of his most characteristic gifts with supreme virtuosity. He is always the poet of variety, of varying attitudes towards life and varying tones of voice. Some of his finest work is in what might be called the poetry of transitions: movements from one fictional world to another, with an utterly different atmosphere. In this conclusion, we are led from the sinister world of the actual story back to the cheerful harmony of the pilgrimage that frames it through a daring series of modulations of feeling. Each shift is surprising, and causes a reassessment of what has preceded; yet each is convincing and unmistakably solid in itself. With each shift we are moved further away from the absorbing horrors of the story, and it takes its place eventually as only one view of a life that can finally be contemplated with sane good humour.

# NOTE ON THE TEXT

The text which follows is based upon that of F. N. Robinson (*The Complete Works of Geoffrey Chaucer*, 2nd ed., 1957). The punctuation has been revised, with special reference to the exclamation marks. Spelling has been partly rationalized, by substituting *i* for *y* wherever the change aids the modern reader and does not affect the semantic value of the word. Thus *smylyng* becomes 'smiling', and *nyghtyngale* 'nightingale', but *wyn* (wine), *lyk* (like), and *fyr* (fire) are allowed to stand.

No accentuation has been provided in this text, for two reasons. First, because it produces a page displeasing to the eye; secondly, because it no longer seems necessary or entirely reliable in the light of modern scholarship. It is not now thought that the later works of Chaucer were written in a ten-syllable line from which no variation was permissible. The correct reading of a line of Chaucer is now seen to be more closely related to the correct reading of a comparable line of prose with phrasing suited to the rhythms of speech. This allows the reader to be more flexible in his interpretation of the line, and makes it unreasonably pedantic to provide a rigid system of accentuation.

## NOTE ON PRONUNCIATION

These equivalences are intended to offer only a rough guide. For further detail, see *An Introduction to Chaucer*.

### SHORT VOWELS

*ă* represents the sound now written *u*, as in 'cut'

*ě* as in modern 'set'

*ĭ* as in modern 'is'

*ŏ* as in modern 'top'

*ŭ* as in modern 'put' ( not as in 'cut')

final -*e* represents the neutral vowel sound in '*a*bout' or 'attent*io*n'. It is silent when the next word in the line begins with a vowel or an *h*.

# Note on the Text

*ā* as in modern 'car' (not as in 'name')

*ē* (open—i.e. where the equivalent modern word is spelt with *ea*) as in modern 'there'

*ē* (close—i.e. where the equivalent modern word is spelt with *ee* or *e*) represents the sound now written *a* as in 'take'

*ī* as in modern 'machine' (not as in 'like')

*ō* (open—i.e. where the equivalent modern vowel is pronounced as in 'br*o*ther', 'm*oo*d', or 'g*oo*d') represents the sound now written *aw* as in 'fawn'

*ō* (close—i.e. where the equivalent modern vowel is pronounced as in 'road') as in modern 'note'

*ū* as in French *tu* or German *Tür*

## DIPHTHONGS

*ai* and *ei* both roughly represent the sound now written *i* or *y* as in 'die' or 'dye'

*au* and *aw* both represent the sound now written *ow* or *ou* as in 'now' or 'pounce'

*ou* and *ow* have two pronunciations: as in *through* where the equivalent modern vowel is pronounced as in 'through' or 'mouse'; and as in *pounce* where the equivalent modern vowel is pronounced as in 'know' or 'thought'

## WRITING OF VOWELS AND DIPHTHONGS

A long vowel is often indicated by doubling, as in *roote* or *eek*. The *ŭ* sound is sometimes represented by an *o* as in *yong*. The *au* sound is sometimes represented by an *a*, especially before *m* or *n*, as in *cha(u)mbre* or *cha(u)nce*.

## CONSONANTS

Largely as in modern English, except that many consonants now silent were still pronounced. *Gh* was pronounced as in Scottish 'lo*ch*', and both consonants should be pronounced in such groups as the following: '*gn*acchen', '*kn*ave', 'wor*d*', 'fo*lk*', '*wr*ong'.

# THE PORTRAIT OF THE PARDONER

From *The General Prologue*, lines 671–716

With him ther rood a gentil PARDONER
Of Rouncivale, his freend and his compeer,
That streight was comen fro the court of Rome.
Ful loude he soong 'Com hider, love, to me!'
This Somonour bar to him a stif burdoun;
Was nevere trompe of half so greet a soun.
This Pardoner hadde heer as yelow as wex,
But smothe it heeng as dooth a strike of flex;
By ounces henge his lokkes that he hadde,
And therwith he his shuldres overspradde;
But thinne it lay, by colpons oon and oon.
But hood, for jolitee, wered he noon,
For it was trussed up in his walet.
Him thoughte he rood al of the newe jet;
Dischevelee, save his cappe, he rood al bare.
Swiche glaringe eyen hadde he as an hare.
A vernicle hadde he sowed upon his cappe.
His walet lay biforn him in his lappe,
Bretful of pardoun, comen from Rome al hoot.
A voys he hadde as smal as hath a goot.
No berd hadde he, ne nevere sholde have;
As smothe it was as it were late shave.
I trowe he were a gelding or a mare.
But of his craft, fro Berwik into Ware,
Ne was ther swich another pardoner.

For in his male he hadde a pilwe-beer,
Which that he seyde was Oure Lady veil:
He seyde he hadde a gobet of the seil
That Seint Peter hadde, whan that he wente
Upon the see, til Jhesu Crist him hente.
He hadde a crois of latoun ful of stones,
And in a glas he hadde pigges bones.
But with thise relikes, whan that he fond
A povre person dwellinge upon lond,
Upon a day he gat him moore moneye
Than that the person gat in monthes tweye;
And thus, with feyned flaterye and japes,
He made the person and the peple his apes.
But trewely to tellen atte laste,
He was in chirche a noble ecclesiaste.
Wel koude he rede a lessoun of a storie,
But alderbest he song an offertorie;
For wel he wiste, whan that song was songe,
He moste preche and wel affile his tonge
To winne silver, as he ful wel koude;
Therefore he song the murierly and loude.

Frame narrative

# THE INTRODUCTION TO
# THE PARDONER'S TALE

Oure Hooste gan to swere as he were wood;
'Harrow!' quod he, 'by nailes and by blood!
This was a fals cherl and a fals justise.
As shameful deeth as herte may devise
Come to thise juges and hire advocats!
Algate this sely maide is slain, allas!
Allas, to deere boughte she beautee!
Wherfore I seye al day that men may see
That yiftes of Fortune and of Nature
Been cause of deeth to many a creature.                    10
Hire beautee was hire deth, I dar wel sayn.
Allas, so pitously as she was slain!
Of bothe yiftes that I speke of now
Men han ful ofte moore for harm than prow.
But trewely, myn owene maister deere,
This is a pitous tale for to heere.
But nathelees, passe over, is no fors.
I pray to God so save thy gentil cors,
And eek thine urinals and thy jurdones,
Thyn ypocras, and eek thy galiones,                        20
And every boyste ful of thy letuarie;
God blesse hem, and oure lady Seinte Marie.
So moot I theen, thou art a propre man,
And lyk a prelat, by Seint Ronyan!
Seyde I nat wel? I kan nat speke in terme;
But wel I woot thou doost myn herte to erme,
That I almoost have caught a cardynacle.

By Corpus bones! but I have triacle,
Or elles a draughte of moiste and corny ale,
30    Or but I heere anon a myrie tale,
Myn herte is lost for pitee of this maide.
Thou beel ami, thou Pardoner,' he saide,
'Telle us som mirthe or japes right anon.'

'It shal be doon,' quod he, 'by Seint Ronyon!
But first,' quod he, 'heere at this alestake
I wol bothe drinke, and eten of a cake.'

But right anon thise gentils gonne to crye,
'Nay, lat him telle us of no ribaudye!
Telle us som moral thing, that we may leere
40    Som wit, and thanne wol we gladly heere.'

'I graunte, ywis,' quod he, 'but I moot thinke
Upon som honest thing while that I drinke.'

# THE PARDONER'S PROLOGUE

'Lordinges,' quod he, 'in chirches whan I preche,
I peyne me to han an hauteyn speche,
And ringe it out as round as gooth a belle,
For I kan al by rote that I telle.
My theme is alwey oon, and evere was—
*Radix malorum est Cupiditas.*

First I pronounce whennes that I come,
And thanne my bulles shewe I, alle and some.          50
Oure lige lordes seel on my patente,
That shewe I first, my body to warente,
That no man be so boold, ne preest ne clerk,
Me to destourbe of Cristes hooly werk.
And after that thanne telle I forth my tales.
Bulles of popes and of cardinales,
Of patriarkes and bishopes I shewe,
And in Latin I speke a wordes fewe,
To saffron with my predicacioun,
And for to stire hem to devocioun.                   60
Thanne shewe I forth my longe cristal stones,
Ycrammed ful of cloutes and of bones,—
Relikes been they, as wenen they echoon.
Thanne have I in latoun a sholder-boon
Which that was of an hooly Jewes sheep.
"Goode men," I seye, "taak of my wordes keep;
If that this boon be wasshe in any welle,
If cow, or calf, or sheep, or oxe swelle
That any worm hath ete, or worm ystonge,
Taak water of that welle and wassh his tonge,        70
And it is hool anon; and forthermoore,

57

Of pokkes and of scabbe and every soore
Shal every sheep be hool that of this welle
Drinketh a draughte. Taak kep eek what I telle:
If that the good-man that the beestes oweth
Wol every wyke, er that the cok him croweth,
Fastinge, drinken of this welle a draughte,
As thilke hooly Jew oure eldres taughte,
His beestes and his stoor shal multiplie.

80      And, sires, also it heeleth jalousie;
For though a man be falle in jalous rage,
Lat maken with this water his potage,
And nevere shal he moore his wif mistriste,
Though he the soothe of hir defaute wiste,
Al had she taken prestes two or thre.

Heere is a miteyn eek, that ye may se.
He that his hand wol putte in this mitayn,
He shal have multiplying of his grain,
Whan he hath sowen, be it whete or otes,
90    So that he offre pens, or elles grotes. *[so long as they pay]*

Goode men and wommen, o thing warne I yow:
If any wight be in this chirche now
That hath doon sinne horrible, that he
Dar nat for shame of it yshriven be, *confessed*
Or any womman, be she yong or old,
That hath ymaad hir housbonde cokewold,
Swich folk shal have no power ne no grace
To offren to my relikes in this place.
And whoso findeth him out of swich blame,
100   He wol come up and offre in Goddes name,
And I assoille him by the auctoritee *absolve*
Which that by bulle ygraunted was to me."

By this gaude have I wonne, yeer by yeer, *trick*

An hundred mark sith I was pardoner.
I stonde lyk a clerk in my pulpet,
And whan the lewed peple is doun yset,
I preche so as ye han herd bifoore,
And telle an hundred false japes moore.
Thanne peyne I me to strecche forth the nekke,
And est and west upon the peple I bekke,                110
As dooth a dowve sittinge on a berne.
Mine handes and my tonge goon so yerne
That it is joye to se my bisynesse.
Of avarice and of swich cursednesse
Is al my preching, for to make hem free
To yeven hir pens, and namely unto me.
For myn entente is nat but for to winne,
And nothing for correccioun of sinne.
I rekke nevere, whan that they been beried,
Though that hir soules goon a-blakeberied.               120
For certes, many a predicacioun
Comth ofte time of yvel entencioun;
Som for plesance of folk and flaterye,
To been avaunced by ypocrisye,
And som for veyne glorie, and som for hate.
For whan I dar noon oother weyes debate,
Thanne wol I stinge him with my tonge smerte
In preching, so that he shal nat asterte
To been defamed falsly, if that he
Hath trespased to my bretheren or to me.                130
For though I telle noght his propre name,
Men shal wel knowe that it is the same
By signes, and by othere circumstances.
Thus quyte I folk that doon us displesances;
Thus spitte I out my venym under hewe

Of hoolinesse, to semen hooly and trewe.
But shortly myn entente I wol devise:
I preche of no thing but for coveitise.     *I only preech against greed*
Therfore my theme is yet, and evere was,

140    *Radix malorum est Cupiditas.*
Thus kan I preche again that same vice
Which that I use, and that is avarice.
But though myself be gilty in that sinne,
Yet kan I maken oother folk to twynne
From avarice, and soore to repente.
But that is nat my principal entente;
I preche nothing but for coveitise.     *I only preech for my own greed.*
Of this mateere it oghte ynogh suffise.

Thanne telle I hem ensamples many oon

150    Of olde stories longe time agoon.
For lewed peple loven tales olde;
Swiche thinges kan they wel reporte and holde.
What, trowe ye that whiles I may preche,
And winne gold and silver for I teche,
That I wol live in poverte wilfully?
Nay, nay, I thoghte it nevere, trewely!
For I wol preche and begge in sondry landes;
I wol nat do no labour with mine handes,
Ne make baskettes, and live therby,

160    By cause I wol nat beggen idelly.
I wol noon of the apostles countrefete;
*modal verb of obligation*     I wol have moneie, wolle, chese, and whete,
Al were it yeven of the povereste page,
Or of the povereste widwe in a village,
Al sholde hir children sterve for famine.
Nay, I wol drinke licour of the vine,
And have a joly wenche in every toun.

60

But herkneth, lordinges, in conclusioun:
Youre liking is that I shal telle a tale.
Now have I dronke a draughte of corny ale,          170
By God, I hope I shal yow telle a thing
That shal by reson been at youre liking.
For though myself be a ful vicious man,
A moral tale yet I yow telle kan,
Which I am wont to preche for to winne.
Now hoold youre pees! my tale I wol biginne.'

very authoritive

# THE PARDONER'S TALE

In Flaundres whilom was a compaignye
Of yonge folk that haunteden folye,
As riot, hasard, stywes, and tavernes,
Where as with harpes, lutes, and giternes,          180
They daunce and pleyen at dees bothe day and night,
And eten also and drinken over hir might,
Thurgh which they doon the devel sacrifise
Withinne that develes temple, in cursed wise,
By superfluitee abhominable.
Hir othes been so grete and so dampnable
That it is grisly for to heere hem swere.
Oure blissed Lordes body they totere—
Hem thoughte that Jewes rente him noght ynough;
And ech of hem at otheres sinne lough.             190
And right anon thanne comen tombesteres
Fetys and smale, and yonge frutesteres,
Singeres with harpes, baudes, wafereres,
Whiche been the verray develes officeres
To kindle and blowe the fyr of lecherye,
That is annexed unto glotonye.
The hooly writ take I to my witnesse
That luxurie is in wyn and dronkenesse.
Lo, how that dronken Looth, unkindely,
Lay by his doghtres two, unwitingly;               200
So dronke he was, he nyste what he wroghte.
Herodes, whoso wel the stories soghte,
Whan he of wyn was repleet at his feeste,
Right at his owene table he yaf his heeste
To sleen the Baptist John, ful giltelees.

Senec seith a good word doutelees; *undoubtedly*

He seith he kan no difference finde *know / provide for*

Bitwix a man that is out of his minde *between*

And a man which that is dronkelewe, *Drunk*

210　But that woodnesse, yfallen in a shrewe, *madness / occurring*

*endures*　Persevereth lenger than doth dronkenesse. *longer* *rouge*

O glotonye, ful of cursednesse!

O cause first of oure confusioun!

O original of oure dampnacioun, *origin*

Til Crist hadde boght us with his blood again! *redeemed*

Lo, how deere, shortly for to sayn, *dear*

Aboght was thilke cursed vileynye— *paid for / that / the* *wickedness*

Corrupt was al this world for glotonye.

Adam oure fader, and his wyf also, *father*

220　Fro Paradis to labour and to wo

Were driven for that vice, it is no drede. *There is no doubt*

For whil that Adam fasted, as I rede, *read*

He was in Paradis; and whan that he

Eet of the fruit deffended on the tree,

Anon he was out cast to wo and peyne. *At once / pain*

O glotonye, on thee wel oghte us pleyne! *(jokes?)*

O, wiste a man how manye maladies *know*

Folwen of excesse and of glotonies, *Follow*

He wolde been the moore mesurable

230　Of his diete, sittinge at his table. *Food and drink*

Allas, the shorte throte, the tendre mouth,

Maketh that est and west and north and south,

In erthe, in eir, in water, men to swinke *labour*

To gete a glotoun deyntee mete and drinke. *delicate*

Of this matiere, o Paul, wel kanstow trete: *matter / deal with*

'Mete unto wombe, and wombe eek unto mete, *food / also*

Shal God destroyen bothe,' as Paulus seith.

*Were preying on* *St Paul*

Allas, a foul thing is it, by my feith,
To seye this word, and fouler is the dede,  *say / deed (act)*
Whan man so drinketh of the white and rede        240
That of his throte he maketh his privee,  *causes / secret*
Thurgh thilke cursed superfluitee.
    The apostel weping seith ful pitously,
'Ther walken manye of whiche yow toold have I—
I seye it now weping, with pitous vois—
That they been enemys of Cristes crois,
Of whiche the ende is deeth, wombe is hir god.'
O wombe! O bely! O stinking cod,
Fulfilled of dong and of corrupcioun!
At either ende of thee foul is the soun.        250
How greet labour and cost is thee to finde!
Thise cookes, how they stampe, and streyne, and
        grinde,
And turnen substaunce into accident,
To fulfille al thy likerous talent!
Out of the harde bones knokke they
The mary, for they caste noght awey
That may go thurgh the golet softe and swoote.
Of spicerie of leef and bark and roote
Shal been his sauce ymaked by delit,
To make him yet a newer appetit.        260
But certes, he that haunteth swiche delices
Is deed, whil that he liveth in tho vices.
    A lecherous thing is wyn, and dronkenesse
Is ful of striving and of wrecchednesse.
O dronke man, disfigured is thy face,
Sour is thy breeth, foul artow to embrace,
And thurgh thy dronke nose semeth the soun
As though thou seydest ay 'Sampsoun, Sampsoun!'

And yet, God woot, Sampsoun drank nevere no wyn.
270 Thou fallest as it were a stiked swyn;
Thy tonge is lost, and al thyn honeste cure;
For dronkenesse is verray sepulture
Of mannes wit and his discrecioun.
In whom that drinke hath dominacioun
He kan no conseil kepe, it is no drede.
Now kepe yow fro the white and fro the rede,
And namely fro the white wyn of Lepe,
That is to selle in Fisshstrete or in Chepe.
This wyn of Spaigne crepeth subtilly
280 In othere wines, growinge faste by,
Of which ther riseth swich fumositee
That whan a man hath dronken draughtes thre,
And weneth that he be at hoom in Chepe,
He is in Spaigne, right at the toune of Lepe—
Nat at the Rochele, ne at Burdeux toun;
And thanne wol he seye 'Sampsoun, Sampsoun!'
But herkneth, lordinges, o word, I yow preye,
That alle the soverein actes, dar I seye,
Of victories in the Olde Testament,
290 Thurgh verray God, that is omnipotent,
Were doon in abstinence and in preyere.
Looketh the Bible, and ther ye may it leere.
Looke, Attilla, the grete conquerour,
Deyde in his sleep with shame and dishonour,
Bledinge ay at his nose in dronkenesse.
A capitain sholde live in sobrenesse.
And over al this, aviseth yow right wel
What was comaunded unto Lamuel—
Nat Samuel, but Lamuel, seye I;
300 Redeth the Bible, and finde it expresly

Of wyn-yeving to hem that han justise.
Namoore of this, for it may wel suffise.

And now that I have spoken of glotonye,
Now wol I yow deffenden hasardrye.
Hasard is verray mooder of lesinges,
And of deceite, and cursed forsweringes,
Blaspheme of Crist, manslaughtre, and wast also
Of catel and of time; and forthermo,
It is repreeve and contrarie of honour
For to ben holde a commune hasardour.                310
And ever the hyer he is of estaat,
The moore is he yholden desolaat.
If that a prince useth hasardrye,
In alle governaunce and policye
He is, as by commune opinioun,
Yholde the lasse in reputacioun.

Stilboun, that was a wys embassadour,
Was sent to Corinthe, in ful greet honour,
Fro Lacidomye, to make hire alliaunce.
And whan he cam, him happede, par chaunce,          320
That alle the gretteste that were of that lond,
Pleyinge atte hasard he hem fond.
For which, as soone as it mighte be,
He stal him hoom again to his contree,
And seyde, 'Ther wol I nat lese my name,
Ne I wol nat take on me so greet defame,
Yow for to allie unto none hasardours.
Sendeth othere wise embassadours;
For, by my trouthe, me were levere die
Than I yow sholde to hasardours allye.              330
For ye, that been so glorious in honours,
Shul nat allyen yow with hasardours

67

As by my wil, ne as by my tretee.'
This wise philosophre, thus seyde hee.

　　Looke eek that to the king Demetrius,
The king of Parthes, as the book seith us,
Sente him a paire of dees of gold in scorn,
For he hadde used hasard ther-biforn;
For which he heeld his glorie or his renoun
340　At no value or reputacioun.
Lordes may finden oother maner pley
Honest ynough to drive the day awey.

　　Now wol I speke of othes false and grete
A word or two, as olde bookes trete.
Gret swering is a thing abhominable,
And fals swering is yet moore reprevable.
The heighe God forbad swering at al,
Witnesse on Mathew; but in special
Of swering seith the hooly Jeremye,
350　'Thou shalt swere sooth thine othes, and nat lie,
And swere in doom, and eek in rightwisnesse';
But idel swering is a cursednesse.
Bihoold and se that in the firste table
Of heighe Goddes heestes honurable,
Hou that the seconde heeste of him is this:
'Take nat my name in idel or amis.'
Lo, rather he forbedeth swich swering
Than homicide or many a cursed thing;
I seye that, as by ordre, thus it stondeth;
360　This knoweth, that his heestes understondeth,
How that the seconde heeste of God is that.
And forther over, I wol thee telle al plat,
That vengeance shal nat parten from his hous
That of his othes is to outrageous.

'By Goddes precious herte,' and 'By his nailes,'
And 'By the blood of Crist that is in Hayles,
Sevene is my chaunce, and thyn is cynk and treye!
'By Goddes armes, if thou falsly pleye,
This daggere shal thurghout thyn herte go!'—
This fruit cometh of the bicched bones two,                    370
Forswering, ire, falsnesse, homicide.
Now, for the love of Crist, that for us dyde,
Lete youre othes, bothe grete and smale.
But, sires, now wol I telle forth my tale.

  Thise riotoures thre of whiche I telle,
Longe erst er prime rong of any belle,
Were set hem in a taverne for to drinke,
And as they sat, they herde a belle clinke
Biforn a cors, was caried to his grave.
That oon of hem gan callen to his knave:                       380
'Go bet,' quod he, 'and axe redily
What cors is this that passeth heer forby;
And looke that thou reporte his name weel.'

  'Sire,' quod this boy, 'it nedeth never-a-deel;
It was me toold er ye cam heer two houres.
He was, pardee, an old felawe of youres;
And sodeynly he was yslain to-night,
Fordronke, as he sat on his bench upright.
Ther cam a privee theef men clepeth Deeth,
That in this contree al the peple sleeth,                      390
And with his spere he smoot his herte atwo,
And wente his wey withouten wordes mo.
He hath a thousand slain this pestilence.
And, maister, er ye come in his presence,
Me thinketh that it were necessarie
For to be war of swich an adversarie.

69

Beth redy for to meete him everemoore;
Thus taughte me my dame; I sey namoore.'
'By seinte Marie,' seyde this taverner,
'The child seith sooth, for he hath slain this yeer,
Henne over a mile, withinne a greet village,
Bothe man and womman, child, and hine, and page;
I trowe his habitacioun be there.
To been avised greet wisdom it were,
Er that he dide a man a dishonour.'

'Ye, Goddes armes!' quod this riotour,
'Is it swich peril with him for to meete?
I shal him seke by wey and eek by strete,
I make avow to Goddes digne bones!
Herkneth, felawes, we thre been al ones;
Lat ech of us holde up his hand til oother,
And ech of us bicomen otheres brother,
And we wol sleen this false traitour Deeth.
He shal be slain, he that so manye sleeth,
By Goddes dignitee, er it be night.'

Togidres han thise thre hir trouthes plight
To live and dien ech of hem for oother,
As though he were his owene ybore brother.
And up they stirte, al dronken in this rage,
And forth they goon towardes that village
Of which the taverner hadde spoke biforn.
And many a grisly ooth thanne han they sworn,
And Cristes blessed body al torente—
Deeth shal be deed, if that they may him hente.

Whan they han goon nat fully half a mile,
Right as they wolde han troden over a stile,
An oold man and a povre with hem mette.
This olde man ful mekely hem grette,

70

And seyde thus, 'Now, lordes, God yow see!'
　　The proudeste of thise riotoures three　　　　430
Answerde again, 'What, carl, with sory grace!
Why artow al forwrapped save thy face?
Why livestow so longe in so greet age?'
　　This olde man gan looke in his visage,
And seyde thus: 'For I ne kan nat finde
A man, though that I walked into Inde,
Neither in citee ne in no village,
That wolde chaunge his youthe for myn age;
And therfore moot I han myn age stille,
As longe time as it is Goddes wille.　　　　440
Ne Deeth, allas, ne wol nat han my lyf.
Thus walke I, lyk a restelees kaitif,
And on the ground, which is my moodres gate,
I knokke with my staf, bothe erly and late,
And seye, "Leeve mooder, leet me in!
Lo how I vanisshe, flessh and blood and skin!
Allas! whan shul my bones been at reste?
Mooder, with yow wolde I chaunge my cheste
That in my chambre longe time hath be,
Ye, for an heyre clowt to wrappe in me."　　　450
But yet to me she wol nat do that grace,
For which ful pale and welked is my face.
　　But sires, to yow it is no curteisye
To speken to an old man vileynye,
But he trespasse in word, or elles in dede.
In Hooly Writ ye may yourself wel rede:
"Agains an oold man, hoor upon his heed,
Ye sholde arise;" wherfore I yeve yow reed,
Ne dooth unto an oold man noon harm now,
Namoore than that ye wolde men did to yow　　460

In age, if that ye so longe abide.
And God be with yow, where ye go or ride!
I moot go thider as I have to go.'
　'Nay, olde cherl, by God, thou shalt nat so,'
Seyde this oother hasardour anon;
'Thou partest nat so lightly, by Seint John!
Thou spak right now of thilke traitour Deeth,
That in this contree alle oure freendes sleeth.
Have heer my trouthe, as thou art his espye,
470　Telle where he is, or thou shalt it abye,
By God, and by the hooly sacrement!
For soothly thou art oon of his assent
To sleen us yonge folk, thou false theef!'
　'Now, sires,' quod he, 'if that yow be so leef
To finde Deeth, turne up this croked wey,
For in that grove I lafte him, by my fey,
Under a tree, and there he wole abide;
Noght for youre boost he wole him no thing hide.
Se ye that ook? Right there ye shal him finde.
480　God save yow, that boghte again mankinde,
And yow amende.' Thus seyde this olde man;
And everich of thise riotoures ran
Til he cam to that tree, and ther they founde
Of florins fine of gold ycoined rounde
Wel ny an eighte busshels, as hem thoughte.
No lenger thanne after Deeth they soughte,
But ech of hem so glad was of that sighte,
For that the florins been so faire and brighte,
That doun they sette hem by this precious hoord.
490　The worste of hem, he spak the firste word.
　'Bretheren,' quod he, 'taak kep what that I seye;
My wit is greet, though that I bourde and pleye.

72

This tresor hath Fortune unto us yiven,
In mirthe and joliftee oure lyf to liven,
And lightly as it comth, so wol we spende.
Ey! Goddes precious dignitee! who wende
To-day that we sholde han so fair a grace?
But mighte this gold be caried fro this place
Hoom to myn hous—or elles unto youres
(For wel ye woot that al this gold is oures)—    500
Thanne were we in heigh felicitee.
But trewely, by daye it may nat bee.
Men wolde seyn that we were theves stronge,
And for oure owene tresor doon us honge.
This tresor moste ycaried be by nighte
As wisely and as slyly as it mighte.
Wherfore I rede that cut among us alle
Be drawe, and lat se wher the cut wol falle;
And he that hath the cut with herte blithe
Shal renne to the town, and that ful swithe,    510
And bringe us breed and wyn ful prively.
And two of us shul kepen subtilly
This tresor wel; and if he wol nat tarie,
Whan it is night, we wol this tresor carie,
By oon assent, where as us thinketh best.'
That oon of hem the cut broghte in his fest,
And bad hem drawe, and looke where it wol falle;
And it fil on the yongeste of hem alle,
And forth toward the toun he wente anon.
And also soone as that he was gon,    520
That oon of hem spak thus unto that oother:
'Thow knowest wel thou art my sworen brother;
Thy profit wol I telle thee anon.
Thou woost wel that oure felawe is agon.

73

And heere is gold, and that ful greet plentee,
That shal departed been among us thre.
But nathelees, if I kan shape it so
That it departed were among us two,
Hadde I nat doon a freendes torn to thee?'

530     That oother answerde, 'I noot how that may be.
He woot wel that the gold is with us tweye;
What shal we doon? What shal we to him seye?'

    'Shal it be conseil?' seyde the firste shrewe,
'And I shal tellen in a wordes fewe
What we shal doon, and bringe it wel aboute.'

    'I graunte,' quod that oother, 'out of doute,
That, by my trouthe, I wol thee nat biwreye.'

    'Now,' quod the firste, 'thou woost wel we be tweye,
And two of us shul strenger be than oon.

540 Looke whan that he is set, that right anoon
Aris as though thou woldest with him pleye,
And I shal rive him thurgh the sides tweye
Whil that thou strogelest with him as in game,
And with thy daggere looke thou do the same;
And thanne shal al this gold departed be,
My deere freend, bitwixen me and thee.
Thanne may we bothe oure lustes all fulfille,
And pleye at dees right at oure owene wille.'
And thus acorded been thise shrewes tweye

550 To sleen the thridde, as ye han herd me seye.

    This yongeste, which that wente to the toun,
Ful ofte in herte he rolleth up and doun
The beautee of thise florins newe and brighte.
'O Lord!' quod he, 'if so were that I mighte
Have al this tresor to myself allone,
Ther is no man that liveth under the trone

Of God that sholde live so murye as I. '
And atte laste the feend, oure enemy,
Putte in his thought that he sholde poison beye,
With which he mighte sleen his felawes tweye;     560
For-why the feend foond him in swich livinge
That he hadde leve him to sorwe bringe.
For this was outrely his fulle entente,
To sleen hem bothe, and nevere to repente.
And forth he gooth, no lenger wolde he tarie,
Into the toun, unto a pothecarie,
And preyde him that he him wolde selle
Som poison, that he mighte his rattes quelle;
And eek ther was a polcat in his hawe,
That, as he seyde, his capouns hadde yslawe,     570
And fain he wolde wreke him, if he mighte,
On vermin that destroyed him by nighte.

  The pothecarie answerde, 'And thou shalt have
A thing that, also God my soule save,
In al this world ther is no creature,
That eten or dronken hath of this confiture
Noght but the montance of a corn of whete,
That he ne shal his lif anon forlete;
Ye, sterve he shal, and that in lasse while
Than thou wolt goon a paas nat but a mile,     580
This poisoun is so strong and violent.'

  This cursed man hath in his hond yhent
This poisoun in a box, and sith he ran
Into the nexte strete unto a man,
And borwed of him large botelles thre;
And in the two his poison poured he;
The thridde he kepte clene for his drinke.
For al the night he shoop him for to swinke

In caryinge of the gold out of that place.
590 And whan this riotour, with sory grace,
Hadde filled with wyn his grete botels thre,
To his felawes again repaireth he.

What nedeth it to sermone of it moore?
For right as they hadde cast his deeth bifoore,
Right so they han him slain, and that anon.
And whan that this was doon, thus spak that oon:
'Now lat us sitte and drinke, and make us merie,
And afterward we wol his body berie.'
And with that word it happed him, par cas,
600 To take the botel ther the poison was,
And drank, and yaf his felawe drinke also,
For which anon they storven bothe two.

But certes, I suppose that Avycen
Wroot nevere in no canon, ne in no fen,
Mo wonder signes of empoisoning
Than hadde thise wrecches two, er hir ending.
Thus ended been thise homicides two,
And eek the false empoisonere also.

O cursed sinne of alle cursednesse!
610 O traitours homicide, O wikkednesse!
O glotonye, luxurie, and hasardrye!
Thou blasphemour of Crist with vileynye
And othes grete, of usage and of pride!
Allas! mankinde, how may it bitide
That to thy creatour, which that the wroghte,
And with his precious herte-blood thee boghte,
Thou art so fals and so unkinde, allas?

Now, goode men, God foryeve yow youre trespas,
And ware yow fro the sinne of avarice!
620 Myn hooly pardoun may yow alle warice,

76

So that ye offre nobles or sterlinges,
Or elles silver broches, spoones, ringes.
Boweth youre heed under this hooly bulle!
Cometh up, ye wives, offreth of youre wolle!
Youre names I entre heer in my rolle anon;
Into the blisse of hevene shul ye gon.
I yow assoille by myn heigh power,
Yow that wol offre, as clene and eek as cleer
As ye were born.—And lo, sires, thus I preche.
And Jhesu Crist, that is oure soules leche,                 630
So graunte yow his pardoun to receive,
For that is best; I wol yow nat deceive.

   But sires, o word forgat I in my tale:
I have relikes and pardoun in my male
As faire as any man in Engelond,
Whiche were me yeven by the popes hond.
If any of yow wole, of devocion,
Offren, and han myn absolucion,
Com forth anon, and kneleth heere adoun,
And mekely receiveth my pardoun;                          640
Or elles taketh pardoun as ye wende,
Al newe and fressh at every miles ende,
So that ye offren, alwey newe and newe,
Nobles or pens, whiche that be goode and trewe.
It is an honour to everich that is heer
That ye mowe have a suffisant pardoneer
T'assoille yow, in contree as ye ride,
For aventures whiche that may bitide.
Paraventure ther may fallen oon or two
Doun of his hors, and breke his nekke atwo.               650
Looke which a seuretee is it to yow alle
That I am in youre felaweshipe yfalle,

77                          **4-2**

That may assoille yow, bothe moore and lasse,
Whan that the soule shal fro the body passe.
I rede that oure Hoost heere shal biginne,
For he is moost envoluped in sinne.
Com forth, sire Hoost, and offre first anon,
And thou shalt kisse the relikes everychon,
Ye, for a grote! Unbokele anon thy purs.

660    'Nay, nay,' quod he, 'thanne have I Cristes curs!
Lat be,' quod he, 'it shal nat be, so theech!
Thou woldest make me kisse thyn olde breech,
And swere it were a relik of a seint,
Though it were with thy fundement depeint!
But, by the crois which that Seint Eleyne fond
I wolde I hadde thy coillons in myn hond
In stide of relikes or of seintuarie.
Lat kutte hem of, I wol thee helpe hem carie;
They shul be shrined in an hogges toord!'

670    This Pardoner answerde nat a word;
So wrooth he was, no word ne wolde he seye.

'Now,' quod oure Hoost, 'I wol no lenger pleye
With thee, ne with noon oother angry man.'
But right anon the worthy Knight bigan,
Whan that he saugh that al the peple lough,
'Namoore of this, for it is right ynough.
Sire Pardoner, be glad and myrie of cheere;
And ye, sire Hoost, that been to me so deere,
I prey yow that ye kisse the Pardoner.

680    And Pardoner, I prey thee, drawe thee neer,
And, as we diden, lat us laughe and pleye.'
Anon they kiste, and riden forth hir weye.

# NOTES

1–16. The Host is referring to the tale just told by the Physician, in which a wicked magistrate (*fals justise*) attempted, with the help of a *fals cherl*, to seduce the beautiful and virtuous daughter of a knight, but was prevented by her father's killing her. Here and elsewhere, Harry Bailly responds to the tales told by the pilgrims with a ready flow of emotion.

1. *as* 'as if'.

2. *by nailes and by blood* An oath by the nails with which Christ was fastened to the cross (or possibly His own finger-nails) and by the blood which He shed on it. Here and in line 28 below we are already being prepared for the blasphemies of *The Pardoner's Tale*.

4. *herte* 'the human mind'.

5. *thise* 'all such'.

7. *to deere boughte she beautee* 'she paid too high a price for her beauty'.

8. *al day* 'always'.

9. *yiftes of Fortune and of Nature* The gifts of Nature were natural endowments of the mind and body (e.g. intelligence and beauty); those of Fortune were outward circumstances such as wealth and social rank. The girl in *The Physician's Tale* possessed both.

13–14. 'People very often receive more harm than benefit from both the gifts I am now referring to.'

17. *passe over, is no fors* 'let us pass over it, it does not matter'.

19–21. The Host is proudly showing off his knowledge of medical terms, but the word *galiones* has not been found elsewhere, and so perhaps he has made a mistake: he may not know as much as he likes to think. The same is true of the word *cardynacle* in line 27.

22. 'God and our Lady Saint Mary bless them.'

23. 'As I hope to prosper, you are a fine-looking man.' *So moot I theen* is a common asseveration, with no exact equivalent in modern speech.

24. *Ronyan* It is not known whether this is St Ronan or St Ninian. The word is pronounced with three syllables here, but with two in line 34 below.

# Notes

25. *in terme* 'in your technical language'. The Host is being mock-modest: he has just been trying to show that he *can* speak *in terme*.

26. *thou doost myn herte to erme* 'you make my heart grieve'.

28. *by Corpus bones!* 'by the bones of Christ's body!'. This is a common oath of Harry's. *But* here is 'unless'.

32. *beel ami* 'good fellow'. A courteous address, taken from the French, the language of medieval courtliness, and perhaps used ironically here.

37–40. Chaucer, like other medieval writers, normally assumes that literary taste follows class distinction; *gentils* (aristocratic people, such as the Knight, the Squire, the Prioress, etc.) will prefer *som moral thing*, while a *cherl* (a person of low rank, such as the Pardoner or Miller) will prefer *ribaudye* (filth).

42. *that* Used redundantly, as here, in many relative constructions. Compare *whennes that I come* in line 49 and *Which that was of an hooly Jewes sheep* in line 65.

44–5. 'I take pains to speak loudly, and to make my sermon ring out as sonorously as a bell.' There is perhaps an unspoken irony in the use of a bell, a religious warning, as a simile to describe something irreligious; compare the remark that the Monk's bridle jingled in the wind as loudly and clearly as the chapel bell (*General Prologue*, 170–1).

47. 'My text is always the same, and always has been.' *Theme* is a technical term of the medieval *ars praedicandi*.

48. 'The desire of money is the root of all evils' (St Paul's first Epistle to Timothy 6:10).

50. *bulles* 'official documents with seals attached'.
    *Alle and some* 'each and every one'.

51. *oure lige lordes seel* This refers to the seal of the bishop who licensed the Pardoner.

52. *my body to warente* 'to protect myself'.

55. *telle I forth my tales* 'I repeat what I have to say'.

56–7. After establishing his right to preach with a presumably genuine document, the Pardoner goes on to dazzle his audience with others which are more likely to be forgeries.

59. *to saffron with my predicacioun* 'with which to give flavour and colour to my sermon'. Saffron is a plant still used in cooking to give a yellow colour and a distinctive taste. The culinary metaphor is a good sign of the Pardoner's attitude towards his sermons: he thinks of them as dishes concocted to impress his congregation.

# Notes

60. *hem* A wealth of contempt is expressed in this single word, the first reference to his congregation.

61. *cristal stones* Glass boxes, such as religious relics are still sometimes kept in.

64. *latoun* This is an alloy of copper and zinc.

65. *an hooly Jewes sheep* The holy Jew was no doubt meant to suggest some Old Testament figure.

69. 'That has eaten or been stung by any creeping creature.' *Worm* was used in Chaucer's time to refer to snakes or insects as well as worms.

72. *of pokkes and of scabbe* These are skin-diseases of sheep.

75. 'If the householder who owns the animals.'

81. *jalous rage* 'a frenzy of jealousy'.

82. 'Let his soup be made with this water.'

85. 'Although she had taken two or three priests as her lovers.' In this last few lines the Pardoner has been playing to his audience like an experienced comedian. The suggestion of a 'cure' for jealousy is likely to be met with a murmur of amusement, arising from the assumption that wives *are* unfaithful; the idea that the 'cure' will work even though the husband *knows* of the infidelity will perhaps produce open laughter; and finally the Pardoner cuts across this with his sudden dig at the immorality of priests, to produce a culminating outburst of laughter.

86. *miteyn* A medieval farmer would use a mitten for sowing seed, since this work had to be done by hand.

90. *so that* 'so long as'. Here the Pardoner first lets his *cupiditas* appear openly.

92–8. This apparently altruistic warning will in fact increase the Pardoner's receipts rather than diminish them, because anyone who does not make an offering will naturally be suspected of being in a state of mortal sin.

93. *that he* 'of such a kind that he'.

98. *offren* 'make an offering' (of money or goods).

99. 'And whoever finds himself free from such a fault.'

104. *an hundred mark* One mark was worth 13s. 4d. (that is, two-thirds of £1), and, since in the fourteenth century money was worth much more than it is now, a hundred marks a year would have been an enormous income.

106. *lewed* 'lay'—not *clerks*, such as the Pardoner pretends to be, and therefore ignorant. In the earlier Middle Ages, literacy, and hence learning, had been almost entirely confined

# Notes

to those in ecclesiastical orders.

110–11. One of the many similes taken by Chaucer from country life, an area of experience which was familiar even to town-dwellers in his own day (because even the largest English towns were very small), but which is likely to be less familiar nowadays. Compare *goon a-blakeberied* in line 120 below.

113. *bisynesse* 'how active I am' (not the modern 'business'). The delight expressed here in the completeness or full-bloodedness of an activity is characteristic of Chaucer, and not just of the Pardoner. In *The Canon's Yeoman's Prologue*, for example, he says of the Canon, who has just ridden up at a great pace, 'But it was joye for to seen him swete!'.

117. *nat but for* 'only'.

118. *nothing* 'not at all'. (It has the same meaning in line 147 below.)

119. *nevere* 'not at all'.

120. *goon a-blakeberied* This means to go wandering all over the place, like someone picking blackberries: a euphemistic way of saying that he does not care if they are damned, once he has their money.

123. 'Some in order to please people and flatter them.'

126. *for* This conjunction seems to indicate that the Pardoner is momentarily classing himself with those who preach well out of hatred, even though his main claim is that he preaches for gain. There is certainly an element of blank malignity, evil for its own sake, in his blasphemous way of life.

127. *him* Someone in his imaginary congregation. Compare the contemptuous *hem* in line 60 above. The image of the Pardoner as a poisonous snake is picked up again in the mention of his spitting out venom in line 135 below.

130. *my bretheren* The Pardoner seems to think of pardoners in general as forming a brotherhood, almost as if they belonged to a religious order like the friars. In fact, *quaestores* were accused by Pope Boniface IX of forming associations to deceive the public, so this turn of phrase may be another sign of Chaucer's accuracy.

134. *doon us displesances* 'do things that displease us'.

137. The explicitness about literary purpose and structure found in this line and in line 148 below—saying what one is going to do, and then saying that one has finished doing it—is characteristic of medieval poetry. It arises from the fact that it

82

## Notes

was normally delivered to an audience of listeners (like the pilgrims), who would not possess copies of what they were listening to, and would need to have its internal structural divisions made clear to them. In a written work these could be indicated by paragraphs and sub-headings.

148. 'That ought to be enough on this subject.'

149. *ensamples* Like *theme*, this is a technical term, meaning stories told to illustrate some general truth. *Ensamples* (*exempla*) were extremely common in medieval sermons.

152. *reporte and holde* 'repeat and keep in their minds'. This of course was the main purpose of *ensamples* in preaching, though the Pardoner mentions it as part of his contempt for his congregations.

154. *for I teche* 'through my teaching'.

156. *I thoghte it nevere* 'I have never intended that'.

159. *make baskettes* St Paul the Hermit made baskets for a living, but Chaucer may have confused him with the apostle St Paul, since the Pardoner immediately afterwards says that he is determined not to imitate any of the apostles.

162-7. There is a relish in these details, as the Pardoner boasts of his sensual egotism, into which one cannot help entering. It is indeed this energy in his evil nature which enables Chaucer to make a study in moral corruption partly comic. One might compare Shakespeare's presentation of Richard in *Richard III*.

166. *licour of the vine* 'juice of the grape'—i.e. wine.

172. *by reson* 'if you are reasonable'.

173-4. The paradox that an evil man can tell a tale which is genuinely moral in its effect is striking. See Introduction, pp. 28.

176. *now hoold youre pees* Another sign of a listening audience. Medieval poetry is full of requests for silence and attention, which were very necessary when literature fulfilled a social function as one among many means of communal entertainment.

177. *whilom* This placing of the story in an indefinite past is used at the beginning of many of *The Canterbury Tales*. It is roughly the equivalent of the fairy story 'once upon a time'.

180. *as* This word is redundant.

   *lutes, and giternes* These were both stringed instruments of the same basic type as the modern guitar.

# Notes

182. *over hir might* 'more than they could hold'.

183–5. Here the tavern is presented as a temple of the devil, in which a blasphemous worship is carried on in the form of gluttony.

185. *abhominable* An 'h' was mistakenly introduced into this word, on the assumption that it was taken from the Latin *ab homine*, 'away from (the true nature of) man'. It thus has a stronger sense than now, meaning 'revoltingly unnatural' or 'bestial'.

188–9. Swearing by the different parts of Christ's body was a common form of verbal blasphemy in the Middle Ages, of which many examples are found in *The Pardoner's Prologue and Tale*. There was a recurrent ecclesiastical campaign against it, and it was often represented by its opponents, as here, as a 'recrucifixion' of Christ.

189. *hem thoughte* 'it seemed to them'. Antisemitism was a persistent element in medieval Christianity, and aroused less horror in Chaucer's time than it does now. The Jewish people were held collectively responsible for the murder of Christ, and in England they were isolated into ghettoes, persecuted, heavily taxed, and finally expelled from the country in 1290. Christian antisemitism is expressed exultantly in *The Prioress's Tale*, in which a little Christian boy is brutally murdered by Jews (ritual murder of children was a favourite accusation against them), and his murderers are eventually tortured and killed.

191. *tombesteres* 'dancing-girls'. There is some doubt whether the *-ster* ending (as in the modern *spinster*) always indicated a female person in Middle English. Here, in the light of *fetys and smale*, it clearly does.

194–5. *whiche been...kindle* 'who are the true servants of the devil, charged with kindling'.

196. A main theme of this section on the sins is the interdependence of the sins: to commit one is to commit all the rest, and all are forms of blasphemy. Thus any sin becomes supremely horrifying and fascinatingly important, and the sinner is drawn into the great drama of the universe, in which God and the devil are locked in mortal combat.

197. 'I take the Bible as my witness.'

198. This line is based on a mistranslation of 'hooly writ'. The Latin text (of St Paul's Epistle to the Ephesians 5:18) reads: 'Nolite inebriari vino, in quo est luxuria' ('And be not drunk

# Notes

with wine, wherein is luxury'), but *luxuria* was taken to have
the specialized medieval sense of 'sexual excess'. The reference
to an authoritative text in support of a statement of one's own
is typical of medieval literature, and especially of the medieval
sermon, where the authority is usually Scriptural. A series of
such references follows, and the Pardoner does not take up his
story again until line 375. The 'interlude' is not irrelevant
however; see Introduction, p. 34.

199. *dronken Looth* See Genesis 19:30–6.

202. *whoso wel the stories soghte* 'as anyone who had looked
carefully through the histories would know'. *The stories* may
be the Biblical accounts of Herod and John the Baptist
(Matthew 14 and Mark 6), or possibly the *Historia Evangelica*
of Peter Comestor, a favourite source-book for Scriptural
*exempla*.

205. *ful giltelees* 'although he was completely innocent'.

206. 'Seneca makes a good remark, undoubtedly.' Seneca was
a Latin writer of the first century A.D., a Stoic philosopher
and a dramatist, who was greatly admired in the Middle Ages.
The remark quoted by the Pardoner comes from one of his
letters.

210. *yfallen in a shrewe* 'when it occurs in some miserable
creature'.

212–14. Invocation of a person or thing not actually present is
part of the rhetorical technique of the medieval art of poetry;
the technical name for it is *exclamatio* or *apostrophatio*. The
aim is usually, as here, to stir up emotion in the audience. The
*oure...oure...us* refers to the whole human race, damned, as
the Pardoner goes on to explain, by Adam's sin of gluttony.

215. *boght us with his blood again* 'redeemed us with His
blood'.

221. *it is no drede* 'there is no doubt'.

222. *as I rede* The Pardoner is in fact drawing on a written
source for this idea, which sounds somewhat odd to modern
ears, that the eating of the forbidden fruit could be classified
as an act of gluttony. The source is St Jerome's *Adversus
Jovinianum*.

226. *on thee wel oghte us pleyne* 'we ought indeed to complain
against you'.

227. *wiste a man* 'if one knew'.

231. *the shorte throte* A compressed and concrete way of
referring to the short time during which the food is still

providing enjoyment, before it reaches the stomach. Here and later the Pardoner presents gluttony not as a moral abstraction but in terms of the physical sensations and activities involved in it—the mouth, the gullet, the throat, and the bustling cooks who labour to provide their brief satisfactions. Gluttony, like the other sins he deals with, thus becomes extraordinarily vivid—repulsive in a way which makes the reader's gorge rise, and yet at the same time irresistibly fascinating.

232–3. The grammatical construction is confused by the enumeration of details (east, west, north, south, etc.), so that *maketh that* is followed not by the subjunctive one would expect, but by the infinitive *to swinke*.

236–7. The quotation from St Paul comes from the 1st Epistle to the Corinthians 6:13: 'Meat for the belly, and the belly for the meats: but God shall destroy both it and them'.

240. *white and rede* 'white and red wines' (compare line 276 below).

241. This strikingly contracted image comes from the *Adversus Jovinianum*.

243. *the apostel* This is St Paul again, the Epistle to the Philippians 3:18–19: 'For many walk, of whom I have told you often (and now tell you weeping) that they are enemies of the cross of Christ: Whose end is destruction: whose God is their belly'.

247. *of whiche* 'whose'. In this line gluttony is again treated as a form of blasphemy, as in lines 183–5 above.

248. The irregular rhythm of this line provides for dramatic pauses between the different names for the belly.

251. *is thee to finde* 'it is to provide for you'.

252. *thise* Used to indicate familiarity with the ways of cooks, not to distinguish any particular group of cooks. *Streyne* is perhaps used in a double sense: 'exert themselves' (connecting it with *stampe*) and 'pass things through strainers' (connecting it with *grinde*). The following remarks on gluttony are borrowed from part of the *De Contemptu Mundi*, by Pope Innocent III.

253. A 'metaphysical' image, borrowed from Innocent III, which plays with the technical language of medieval philosophy. In this language *accidents* are external characteristics (e.g. redness, hardness, coldness) and *substaunce* is the supposed essence underlying these. Thus the Pardoner means that the

cooks so completely transform the external qualities of their ingredients that no one could tell what 'substaunce' their dishes are made of. But the line may also include a blasphemous parody of the Catholic doctrine that in the Mass the bread and wine are 'trans-substantiated' into the body and blood of Christ, despite their retaining the 'accidents' of ordinary bread and wine. In Chaucer's own time this doctrine had been denied by John Wyclif, so that it was a controversial matter, to which an allusion would quickly be picked up.

257. When spoken, this line has a repulsively slippery sound, which perfectly conveys a sense of the sliding of soft, rich food down the throat.

259. 'The glutton's sauce shall be made for his delight.'

260. 'To renew his appetite continually.'

261–2. Another quotation from St Paul (1st Epistle to Timothy 5:6): 'For she that liveth in pleasures is dead while she is living'.

263. At this point the Pardoner turns from gluttony in general to speak of the special form of gluttony that leads to drunkenness. There is also a change of tone—essential if the audience's interest is to be held—from portentous denunciation to coarse humour with a more direct appeal.

268. *Sampsoun* An imitation of a drunkard's heavy snoring, which in the next line provides an unexpected and telling moral point.

270. *as it were a stiked swyn* 'like a stuck pig'.

274. *in whom that* 'the man in whom'.

276. *kepe yow fro* 'keep yourselves away from'.

278. Fish Street and Cheapside, both of which still exist, were part of the shopping centre of medieval London. Chaucer's father, who was a wine merchant (hence, no doubt, Chaucer's apparently expert knowledge), lived in Thames Street, from which Fish Street leads out.

*To selle* 'for sale'.

279–80. These lines are perhaps said with a wink. The Pardoner is jokingly suggesting that Spanish wine from *Lepe* is to be found mixed with wine from the South of France (*Rochele* or *Burdeux* in line 285) because the vineyards are close together. In fact it is because the wine merchants dilute expensive French wines with cheap Spanish ones. The result is heady.

281. *fumositee* According to medieval physiology, the contents

# Notes

of the stomach could produce vapours which literally 'went to one's head', and produced dreams or the symptoms of drunkenness.

288. *dar I seye* 'I have no hesitation in saying'.

293. *looke* A common way of introducing an *exemplum*.

293–5. Attila, king of the tribe of Huns, died in bed after a drunken debauch on his wedding night.

300–1. 'Read the Bible, and see what is explicitly said there about giving wine to those who administer justice.' The reference is to Proverbs 31:4–5: 'Give not to kings, O Lamuel, give not wine to kings: because there is no secret where drunkenness reigneth; And lest they drink and forget judgments, and pervert the cause of the children of the poor.'

303–4. The Pardoner is getting into his stride, and is determined to leave no sin mentioned in his story without its sermon.

307–8. The anti-climax of the descent from murder to time-wasting is no doubt deliberate. See Introduction, p. 32.

317–34. This *exemplum*, and the attack on gambling which it illustrates, are both taken from a Latin work by a twelfth-century English writer, the *Policraticus* of John of Salisbury. According to John the ambassador's name was 'Chilon'.

319. *make hire alliaunce* 'make an alliance with the Corinthians'.

329–30. 'For, on my honour, I would rather die than ally you to gamblers.'

336. *the book* The *Policraticus*.

337. *him* This word is redundant.

346. *fals swering* 'swearing oaths that one does not intend to keep'.

348. *Mathew* The reference is to Matthew 5:33–4: 'Again you have heard that it was said to them of old, Thou shalt not forswear thyself: but thou shalt perform thy oaths to the Lord. But I say to you not to swear at all.'

350–1. The quotation is from Jeremiah 4:2: 'And thou shalt swear: As the Lord liveth, in truth and in judgment and in justice.'

351. *in doom* That is, when a formal oath is required, as in a court of law.

353. *firste table* The first tablet of the Law, i.e. the first five of the Ten Commandments given by God to Moses.

355. *seconde heeste* The second according to the Roman Catholic division; the third according to the Protestant division.

359. *as by ordre* 'according to the order of the Commandments'.

# Notes

**360.** 'One who understands His commandments knows.'

**363–4.** From Ecclesiasticus 23:12: 'A man that sweareth much shall be filled with iniquity: and a scourge shall not depart from his house.'

**365.** *nailes* See note on line 2.

**366.** The abbey of Hales in Gloucestershire possessed a phial which was supposed to contain some of Christ's blood.

**367.** This line uses the technical jargon of medieval gambling. In the game of *hasard*, a *chaunce* is a dice-throw which neither loses nor wins, but enables the thrower to have another turn. French numbers (as *cynk* and *treye*) were used for the six faces of the dice.

**370.** *bones two* 'dice'.

**375.** The Pardoner now at last turns back from his sermon to the story which exemplifies the sins he has been preaching against. And once he has started, he leaps to the heart of the story with masterly abruptness. *Of whiche I telle* may be in the future tense ('of whom I am going to tell you'), but the *riotoures* have not been mentioned before, and this opening implies a familiarity which does not really exist.

**376.** *prime* This is one of the seven canonical hours, the times appointed by the Church for prayer. It means about six in the morning, but by mentioning the time Chaucer reminds us of the divine context in which this revelry is set: service begins early in the *develes temple*.

**377.** *were set hem* 'had sat themselves down'.

**378.** A bell was carried along in front of the corpse at a funeral.

**380.** *that oon of hem gan callen* 'one of them called'.

**387.** *to-night* 'this last night'.

**388.** The irregularity of rhythm in this line throws a meaningful emphasis on *fordronke*.

**389–90.** In these lines the long repeated *ee*'s and *th* sounds horribly suggest the slithering approach of death, and at the same time the awed whisper in which the boy mentions him.

**393.** *this pestilence* 'during this plague'. Medieval England was periodically ravaged by plagues—hence the matter-of-factness of this reference.

**401.** *henne over a mile* 'over a mile from here'.

**406.** *Goddes armes* The first of the many oaths by parts of God's body that the Pardoner has warned us to expect.

**408.** *by wey and eek by strete* 'through highways and by-ways'.

# Notes

411. They raise their hands ceremonially as they take the oath of brotherhood.

418. *ybore brother* 'brother by birth'.

425. *nat fully* 'almost'.

426. *wolde han troden* 'were going to step'.

427. On the identity and function in the story of this mysterious old man, see Introduction, pp. 37–40.

431. *with sory grace!* 'bad luck to you!'.

436. *into Inde* This is a common formula in medieval poetry, standing for 'to the end of the earth'.

441–52. Compare Revelation 9:6: 'And in those days men shall seek death and shall not find it. And they shall desire to die: and death shall fly from them'.

443–4. The ground is his mother's gate because the earth is his mother. Thus the tapping of his walking-stick is presented as a request for re-admittance to the earth that bore him.

448–50. The old man means that he wishes he could exchange his *cheste* full of clothes for the shroud in which he will be buried.

453–4. *curteisye . . . vileynye* These words are traditional opposites, meaning the behaviour that one would expect of a courtly person and of an uncultivated lower-class person (a *vilein*) respectively.

457–8. The quotation is from Leviticus 19:32: 'Rise up before the hoary head, and honour the person of the aged man'.

461. For *if* Chaucer may have written *yif*, an older form of the same word which is found in some manuscripts; this would prevent an elision between *age* and *if* from making the line too short. But a hiatus instead of an elision between the two words would provide a significant pause before the sinister irony of the old man's doubt: 'In age—if that ye so longe abide'.

462. More irony: God will indeed be with the revellers, and will pass judgement on them, though they disregard His presence.

463. This line suggests another element in the mystery surrounding the old man: he has a destination, but where is not disclosed.

469. *have heer my trouthe* 'take my word'.

475. *croked wey* The crookedness of the path which will lead them to Death is of course symbolic: it is the path of sin.

480–1. *God save...yow amende* 'God, who redeemed mankind, preserve you and make you better'.

# Notes

484. *florins* Coins worth half a mark, or 6s. 8d.

485. *wel ny an eighte busshels* 'something like eight bushels' (about 300 litres).

493-4. Compare the Host's remark in lines 8–10 that the gifts of Fortune often bring death: the reveller has no grounds for his confidence.

495. 'And we will spend it as easily as it has come to us.' Compare the proverb, 'Lightly come, lightly go'.

498-501. *mighte this gold...thanne were we* 'if this gold might ...then we would be'.

499. His first words betray his immediate thought—to keep the gold for himself—but he quickly corrects them and glosses over his mistake with an assurance that the gold belongs, of course, to all of them.

501. *heigh felicitee* 'supreme happiness'. The phrase has a theological flavour: *felicitee* tends to be applied to the blessedness of heaven, and the reveller is mistaking the nature of true happiness.

504. *doon us honge* 'have us hanged'.

507-8. He is proposing that someone should hold out a number of straws in his hand, each should draw one out, and the person who draws the shortest should have to go and fetch provisions for them. This was a common way of drawing lots in medieval times; it is the method the Host suggests in *The General Prologue* for deciding who should tell the first tale.

508. *lat se wher* 'let us see on whom'.

509. *with herte blithe* The idea seems to be 'willingly, without grumbling about it'; but the phrase is little more than a tag.

515. *by oon assent* 'by agreement among us all'.

516. *that oon* 'one'; compare *that oon* and *that oother* in line 521.

523. *thy profit* 'something that will do you good'.

525. *and that ful greet plentee* 'and a vast amount of it too'.

529. 'Wouldn't I have done you a friendly turn?'

546. *my deere freend* The parenthetic placing of this phrase, along with its long *ee* sounds, effectively suggests cunning.

548. *right at oure owene wille* 'exactly as we please'.

554. *if so were* 'if it should come about'.

563. 'For his fixed intention was definitely.'

569. *polcat* A small animal like a weasel, now rare in England, but more common in Chaucer's time.

571. 'And he was eager to take vengeance if he could.'
572. *vermin* For the chemist this means the rats and the polecat, but the reveller is contemptuously applying the term to his companions, not knowing that they are in fact intending to 'destroy' him.
574. *also God my soule save* 'as I hope to be saved'.
576–8. 'Who, after eating or drinking an amount of this preparation the size of a grain of wheat, will not immediately lose his life.'
579–80. *and that...a mile* 'and that in less time than it will take you to walk a mile at normal speed'. The chemist uses images of a very immediate kind: it is unpleasantly easy to imagine the amount needed of the poison, and the exact time it takes to work.
583. *he ran* This is only one of many indications of violent speed in the Tale. See Introduction, pp. 35–37.
593. *sermone of* 'talk on about'. The word *sermone* does not necessarily imply actual preaching.
597–8. The jaunty rhythm of this couplet is intentionally jarring: the revellers have no idea what fate they are on the brink of.
602. The final stages of the Tale are presented in a deliberately flat, laconic way, and in this line the very syntax conspires to underplay the climax, by mentioning the last two deaths in a subordinate clause, as if they were only an afterthought.
603. *Avycen* Avicenna, the Latinized form of the name of Ibn Sina, the great Arabic philosopher and scientist. He was well known in the West as an authority on medicine.
604. *canon...fen* Avicenna's chief work, the *Book of the Canon in Medicine*, was divided into sections called *fens*, and it often uses the term *canon* in chapter-headings to mean 'rule of procedure'.
610. *traitours homicide* 'murderous betrayers'.
612. *Thou blasphemour* This presumably refers to 'synne', but the Pardoner is now no doubt running his eyes over his audience.
615. *which that the wroghte* 'who made you'.
619. *avarice* The transition is now complete from the unmitigated horror of the Tale itself to the Pardoner's usual roguery.
621. *nobles or sterlinges* i.e. gold or silver.
630–2. For interpretative comment on these lines, see Introduction, pp. 47–48.

# Notes

631. *so graunte* 'grant'.

642. *al newe and fressh* He speaks of pardon as if it were something physically delightful, such as a cake. Compare the description of the Pardoner's wallet in *The General Prologue* as 'Bretful of pardoun, comen from Rome al hoot'.

649–50. He seems to take a positive delight in the possibility: not just one of them may break his neck, but one or two.

651. *looke which a seuretee* 'think what a safeguard'.

652–3. 'That I have fallen into company with you—I who can absolve you, whatever your rank.'

660–9. This coarse outspokenness is characteristic of the Host. He is a powerful man, who is dominated by none of the pilgrims, but only by his wife.

660. *thanne have I Cristes curs* 'may I be cursed by Christ if I do'.

661. *so theech* 'as I may prosper'.

665. St Helena, the mother of Constantine the Great, was supposed to have discovered the actual cross on which Christ was crucified.

666–7. In the *Roman de la Rose* Reason argues that *coilles* (testicles) is no more an improper word than 'relics'. That Chaucer had this passage in mind is confirmed by the fact that this is the earliest recorded use of *coillons* in English.

668. *lat kutte hem of* 'have them cut off'. The Host's coarseness has indeed a sharp edge; Chaucer in *The General Prologue* has said that the Pardoner is 'a gelding or a mare'.

674–81. The Knight is the person of highest secular rank on the pilgrimage, so he is in a position to act as arbitrator in quarrels; and since he is a good-natured man, and takes seriously the responsibilities of his rank, he often does so.

676. *right ynough* 'quite enough'.

679–80. *I prey yow . . . prey thee* According to the manuscript on which this text is based, the Knight addresses the Host with the respectful plural form, and the Pardoner with the familiar singular.

93

# GLOSSARY

*abhominable* unnatural (see
note on l. 185)
*abide* (inf. *abiden*) (l. 461)
endure; (l. 477) wait
*a-blakeberied* wandering about
*aboght* (inf. *abyen*) paid for
*abye* (inf. *abyen*) pay for
*accident* see note on l. 253
*acorded* (inf. *acorden*) come
to an agreement
*actes* deeds
*adoun* down
*advocas* lawyers
*again* (l. 141) against; (l. 431)
back
*agains* in the presence of
*ago(o)n* past; (l. 524) gone
*al* (as conjunction, followed
by subjunctive verb)
although
*alestake* inn signpost
*algate* all the same
*allyen* (sometimes reflexive)
make alliance with
*also* (l. 520) as
*alwey* always
*amende* (inf. *amenden*) make
better, reform
*ami* companion
*amis* wrongly
*annexed* linked
*anon* at once
*artow* art thou
*as* (ll. 1, 543) as if; (l. 179)
such as
*assent* (l. 472) conspiracy;
(l. 515) agreement
*assoille* (inf. *assoillen*) absolve

*asterte* (inf. *asterten*) avoid
*atte* at the
*Attilla* Attila, king of the
Huns
*atwo* in two pieces
*auctoritee* authority
*avaunced* promoted
*aventures* accidents
*avised* (inf. *avisen*) prepared
*aviseth yow* (inf. *avisen*)
consider
*avow* (l. 409) *make avow*
swear
*Avycen* Avicenna
*axe* (inf. *axen*) ask
*ay* always
*bad* (inf. *bidden*) told,
ordered
*baudes* bawds, procurers
*be* (inf. *be(e)n*) been
*be(e)n* be, are
*bekke* (inf. *bekken*) nod the
head
*berie* (inf. *berien*) bury
*berne* barn
*bet* (l. 381) quickly
*beth* (inf. *be(e)n*) be
*beye* (inf. *b(e)yen*) buy
*bicched* cursed
*bicomen* become
*bifoore* before
*biforn* before, in front of
*bigan* (inf. *biginnen*) began
*bihoolde* (inf. *biholden*)
behold, look
*bitide* come to pass
*bitwix* between
*bitwixen* between

# Glossary

*biwreye* (inf. *biwreyen*) give away

*blame* fault

*blaspheme* blasphemy

*blissed* blessed

*blithe* gay

*boght again* (inf. *b(e)yen*) redeemed

*boon* bone

*boost* boasting

*borwed* (inf. *borwen*) borrowed

*botel* bottle

*bo(u)ghte* (inf. *b(e)yen*) (l. 7) paid for; (l. 616) redeemed

*bourde* (inf. *bourden*) joke

*boyste* box

*breech* breeches

*breed* bread

*breke* (inf. *breken*) break

*broches* brooches

*bulle* official document

*Burdeux* Bordeaux

*but* (ll. 28, 30, 455) unless

*cake* loaf of bread

*cam* (inf. *comen*) came

*canon* rule of procedure (see note to l. 604)

*capitain* commander

*capouns* capons (castrated cocks)

*cardynacle* heart-attack

*carl* fellow

*cas, par cas* by chance

*cast* (inf. *casten*) planned

*catel* goods, money

*certes* certainly

*chambre* room, bedroom

*chaunce* (l. 320) *par chaunce* by chance; (l. 367) see note

*chaunge* (inf. *chaungen*) exchange

*cheere* mood

*Chepe* Cheapside

*cherl* villain, lower-class person

*cheste* clothes chest

*citee* city

*cleer* free from sin

*clene* clean

*clepeth* (inf. *clepen*) calls

*clerk* learned person, scholar, or one in holy orders

*clowt* garment; (l. 450) shroud

*clowtes* rags

*cod* bag

*coillons* testicles

*cokewold* cuckold

*comen* (inf. *comen*) came

*commune* (l. 310) notorious; (l. 315) common

*compaignye* company, gang

*comth* (inf. *comen*) comes

*confiture* preparation

*confusioun* ruin

*conseil* secret

*contree* country

*Corinthe* Corinth

*corn* grain

*corny* malty

*corrupt* corrupted

*cors* (l. 18) body; (ll. 379, 382) corpse

*countrefete* (inf. *countrefeten*) imitate

*coveitise* covetousness

*creatour* creator

*crepeth* (inf. *crepen*) creeps

*crois* cross

*croked* crooked

*cure* care

*curteisye* courtesy

*cut* lot(s)

*cynk* five

*dame* mother

*dampnable* damnable
*dampnacioun* damnation
*debate* fight, attack
*dede* deed, act
*deed* dead
*deere* dear
*dees* dice
*deeth* death
*defame* dishonour, disgrace
*defamed* disgraced, slandered
*defaute* fault, lapse
*deffended* (inf. *deffenden*) forbidden
*deffenden* forbid
*delices* delights
*delit* delight
*departed* (inf. *departen*) divided
*depeint* stained
*desolaat* disgraced
*destourbe* (inf. *destourben*) hinder
*destroyed* (inf. *destroyen*) were preying on
*devise* (inf. *devisen*) describe
*deyde* (inf. *deyen*) died
*deyntee* delicate
*diete* food and drink
*digne* noble
*dignitee* glory
*discrecioun* judgement
*dishonour* injury
*doghtres* daughters
*dominacioun* domination
*dong* dung
*doom* judgement
*doon* (infinitive) do, cause; (past participle) done
*dooth* (inf. *doon*) do, does
*doute* doubt
*doutelees* undoubtedly
*dowve* dove, pigeon

*drawe* (inf. *drawen*) drawn
*drede* (ll. 221, 275) *it is no drede* there is no doubt
*dronke(n)* drunk
*dronkelewe* drunk
*dronkenesse* drunkenness
*dyde* (inf. *deyen*) died
*ech* each
*echoon* each one
*eek* also
*eet* (inf. *eten*) ate
*Eleyne* St Helena
*elles* else
*embassadour* ambassador
*empoisonere* poisoner
*empoisoning* poisoning
*ensample* illustrative stories
*entencioun* intention
*entente* purpose
*entre* (inf. *entren*) enter
*envoluped* enveloped
*er* before
*erly* early
*erme* grieve
*erst er* before
*espye* spy
*est* east
*estaat* social rank, position
*eten* (inf. *eten*) eaten
*everemoore* always
*everich* each (one)
*expresly* explicitly
*fader* father
*fain* willingly
*fair* good, fine
*fals* wicked, deceiving, lying
*falsnesse* deceit
*faste* (l. 280) close
*feend* devil
*felawe* companion
*felaweshipe* company
*felicitee* happiness

# Glossary

*fen* section (see note on l. 604)

*fest* fist

*fetys* neat, graceful

*fey* faith

*fil* (inf. *fallen*) fell

*finde* (inf. *finden*) (l. 251) provide for

*Fisshstrete* Fish Street

*Flaundres* Flanders

*florin* coin worth 6s. 8d.

*folwen* follow

*fo(o)nd* (inf. *finden*) found

*for* for, because

*forbedeth* (inf. *forbeden*) forbids

*forby* past

*fordronke* completely drunk

*forgat* (inf. *forgeten*) forgot

*forlete* (inf. *forleten*) lose

*forswering* perjury

*forthermo* furthermore

*forther over* moreover

*for-why* because

*forwrapped* wrapped up

*foryeve* (inf. *foryeven*) forgive

*foul* ugly, disgusting

*free* generous

*fro* from

*frutesteres* fruit-sellers

*ful* very, completely

*fulfilled* filled full

*fumositee* vapour (see note to l. 281)

*fundement* bottom

*galiones* ?drinks named after the physician Galen

*gan* (inf. *ginnen*) began; also used as an auxiliary to indicate the past tense (e.g. *gan callen* in l. 380, 'called')

*gaude* trick

*gentil* noble

*gentils* upper-class people

*giltelees* innocent

*giternes* citterns

*glotonye* gluttony; (l. 228) *glotonies*, cases of gluttony

*glotoun* glutton

*golet* gullet

*gonne* (inf. *ginnen*) began

*good-man* householder

*goon* go, walk

*governaunce* government

*grace* favour, luck

*graunte* (inf. *graunten*) agree; (l. 631) grant

*grete, greet* great, large

*grette* (inf. *greten*) greeted

*gretteste* greatest

*grisly* horrifying

*grote* coin worth 4d.

*habitacioun* dwelling

*han* (inf. *ha(ve)n*) have

*happed(e)* (inf. *happen*) (it) occurred, befell

*harrow!* a cry of distress

*hasardour* gambler

*hasard(rye)* gambling

*haunteden* (inf. *haunten*) practised, gave themselves up to

*haunteth* (inf. *haunten*) practises

*hauteyn* loud

*hawe* yard

*Hayles* Hales

*heed* head

*heeld* (inf. *holden*) considered, rated

*heer* here

*heeste* command(ment)

*heigh(e)* high

## Glossary

*hem* them(selves)

*henne* from here

*hente* (inf. *henten*) seize, catch

*herkneth* (inf. *herkneh*) listen (to)

*Herodes* Herod

*herte* heart

*hevene* heaven

*hewe* colour, appearance

*heyre* (made of) haircloth

*hine* labourer

*hir* their

*hogges* Hog's

*holde* (inf. *holden*) (l. 152) retain; (l. 310) considered

*homicide* (ll. 358, 371) murder; (l. 610) murderous

*homicides* (l. 607) murderers

*hond* hand

*honest* decent; (l. 271) *honeste cure*, care for respectability

*honge* (inf. *hongen*) hang

*honurable* deserving reverence

*hool* cured

*hooly writ* the Bible

*hoom* home

*hoor* grey

*hoord* hoard

*hope* (inf. *hopen*) intend

*idel* vain

*Inde* India

*ire* anger

*japes* (l. 33) jokes; (l. 108) untrue stories

*Jeremye* Jeremiah

*joliftee* gaiety

*jurdones* chamber-pots

*kaitif* prisoner

*kan* (l. 46) know; (l. 527) can

*kanstow?* canst thou?

*ke(e)p* heed, notice

*kepen* guard, keep

*kiste* (inf. *kissen*) kissed

*knave* serving-boy

*kneleth* (inf. *knelen*) kneel

*kutte* (inf. *kutten*) cut

*Lacidomye* Lacedaemon, Sparta

*lafte* (inf. *leven*) left

*Lamuel* Lemuel

*lasse* less

*lat* (inf. *leten*) let

*lat be* give up

*leche* doctor, healer

*lecherous* causing lechery

*leef* desirous

*leere* (inf. *leeren*) learn

*leet* (inf. *leten*) let

*leeve* dear

*lenger* longer

*Lepe* a town in Spain

*lese* (inf. *lesen*) lose

*lesinges* lies

*lete* (inf. *leten*) give up

*letuarie* medicine

*leve* permission

*levere* rather, more willingly

*lewed* lay, ignorant

*licour* juice

*lightly* easily

*likerous* greedy

*livestow?* (inf. *liven*) dost thou live?

*livinge* way of life

*lond* land

*looke* (inf. *looken*) consider (how); (ll. 540, 544) see to it

*Looth* Lot

*lordinges* (ladies and) gentlemen

*lough* (inf. *laughen*) laughed
*lustes* desires
*luxurie* lechery
*lyf* life
*maister* master, sir
*maketh* (inf. *maken*) (l. 232) causes
*male* bag
*man* (l. 240) one
*maner* kind of
*mark* money worth 13s. 4d.
*mary* marrow
*Mathew* St Matthew
*matiere* matter
*mekely* humbly
*men* people, one
*mesurable* (*of*) moderate (in)
*mete* food
*might* (l. 182) capacity
*mirthe* happiness
*mistriste* mistrust
*mitayn, miteyn* mitten
*mo* more
*moiste* fresh
*montance* amount
*mooder* mother
*moore and lasse* (l. 653) whatever your rank
*moot* (l. 23) may; (l. 41) must
*moste* must
*mowe* (inf. *mowen*) may
*murye* happily
*myn* my, mine
*myrie* pleasant, gay
*namely* especially
*namoore* no more
*nat* not
*nathelees* nevertheless
*nay* no
*ne* nor
*nedeth* (inf. *neden*) is necessary

*nekke* neck
*never-a-deel* not at all
*nevere* (l. 119) not at all
*nobles* gold coins worth 6s. 8d.
*noght* nothing, not, not at all
*none, noon* no
*noot* (inf. *witen*) do not know
*nothing* (l. 118) not at all
*ny* nearly
*nyste* (inf. *witen*) did not know
*o* one
*of* (l. 668) off
*officeres* servants
*offren* make an offering
*offreth* (inf. *offren*) offer
*oghte* (inf. *owen*) ought; (l. 226) *oghte us*, we ought
*ones* (l. 410) *al ones* at one
*oon* one
*ooth* oath
*original* origin
*othes* oaths
*out of* (l. 99) free from
*outrely* completely
*over* over, beyond
*owene* own
*oweth* (inf. *owen*) owns
*paas* (l. 580) *goon a paas* walk at normal speed
*page* servant
*paire* set
*paraventure* perhaps
*pardee* indeed
*parten* depart
*partest* (inf. *parten*) (l. 466) shalt depart
*Parthes* Parthians
*patente* licence
*Paul(us)* St Paul
*pens* pennies
*peple* people

99

*persevereth* (inf. *perseveren*)
  lasts, endures
*peyne me* (inf. *peynen*) take
  pains
*pitous(ly)* piteous(ly)
*plat* flatly
*plentee* a large amount
*plesance* giving of pleasure
*pleyen* play, joke
*pleyne (on)* (inf. *pleynen*)
  complain (about), cry out
  (against)
*plighte* (inf. *plighten*) pledged
*pokkes* pocks
*polcat* polecat
*policye* ruling, administration
*potage* soup
*pothecarie* chemist
*povereste* poorest
*povre* poor
*predicacioun* preaching
*prelat* bishop, or other high
  ecclesiastic
*preye* (inf. *preyen*) beg, pray,
  request
*preyere* prayer
*prince* ruler
*privee* (l. 389) secret;
  (l. 241) lavatory
*prively* secretly
*profit* advantage
*pronounce* (inf. *pronouncen*)
  declare
*propre* own
*prow* benefit
*quelle* (inf. *quellen*) kill
*quod* (inf. *quethen*) said
*quyte* (inf. *quyten*) repay
*rage* fit of madness
*rather* sooner, earlier
*rede* (inf. *reden*) read;
  (ll. 507, 655) advise

*redily* quickly
*reed* advice
*rekke* (inf. *rekken*) care
*relik(es)* relic(s)
*renne* (inf. *rennen*) run
*rente* (inf. *renden*) tore
*repaireth* (inf. *repairen*)
  returns
*repleet* full
*reporte* (inf. *reporten*) repeat
*repreeve* shame
*reprevable* shameful
*reputacioun* estimation
*ribaudye* coarseness, filth
*riden* (inf. *riden*) rode
*right* just, quite
*rightwisnesse* righteousness
*riot* debauchery
*riotour* reveller, debauchee
*rive* (inf. *riven*) stab
*Rochele* La Rochelle
*rolle* list
*rong* (inf. *ringen*) rang
*Ronyan* see note to l. 24
*Sampsoun* Samson
*saugh* (inf. *seen*) saw
*save* except
*se(e)* (inf. *seen*) see
*se(e)* (inf. *seen*) (l. 429)
  *God yow see* God keep watch
  over you
*seide* (inf. *seyen*) said
*seint* saint
*seintuarie* casket for relics
*sely* innocent
*Senec* Seneca
*sepulture* burial
*sermone* (inf. *sermonen*) talk
*set(te)* (inf. *sitten*) seated
*seuretee* safeguard
*shape* (inf. *shapen*) arrange
*sholde* (inf. *shullen*) should

## Glossary

*shoop him* (inf. *shapen*) planned
*shortly* briefly
*shrewe* wretch, rogue, scoundrel
*shrined* enshrined
*shul* (inf. *shullen*) shall
*signes* signs; (l. 605) symptoms
*sires* (ladies and) gentlemen
*sith* since; (l. 583) then
*sleen* kill
*sleeth* (inf. *sleeth*) kills
*smale* slim
*smerte* sharply
*smoot* (inf. *smiten*) struck
*sodeynly* suddenly
*soghte* (inf. *sechen*) searched, looked through
*sondry* various
*soore* (l. 72) disease; (l. 145) deeply
*sooth* true
*soothe* truth
*soothly* truly
*sorwe* sorrow
*sory* wretched; (ll. 431, 590) *with sory grace*, bad luck to you (him)
*so that* (ll. 90, 621, 643) so long as
*soun* sound
*soverein* principal, main
*Spaigne* Spain
*spak* (inf. *speken*) spoke, said
*special* particular
*speken* speak, say
*spere* spear
*spicerie* mixture of spices
*staf* stick
*stal him* (inf. *stelen*) stole, went secretly

*sterlinges* silver pennies
*sterve* (inf. *sterven*) die
*stide* (l. 667) *in stide* instead
*stiked* stuck
*Stilboun* Chilon
*stirte* (inf. *sterten*) jumped
*stondeth* (inf. *stonden*) stands
*stoor* livestock
*stories* histories
*storven* (inf. *sterven*) died
*strenger* stronger
*streyne* (inf. *streynen*) strain
*striving* strife, quarrelling
*strogelest* (inf. *stroglen*) strugglest
*stronge* (l. 503) open
*stywes* brothels
*substaunce* see note on l. 253
*subtilly* cunningly
*suffisant* competent
*suffise* (inf. *suffisen*) suffice, be enough
*superfluitee* sensual excess
*suppose* (inf. *supposen*) think
*swere* (inf. *sweren*) swear
*swich(e)* such
*swinke* (inf. *swinken*) labour
*swithe* quickly
*sworen* sworn
*swote* sweetly
*swyn* pig
*taak* (inf. *taken*) take
*table* group of Commandments
*talent* desire
*tarie* (inf. *tarien*) delay
*taverner* inn-keeper
*thanne* then
*the* (pronoun) thee, you
*theech* (inf. *theen*) may I prosper
*theen* prosper
*theme* text

*ther* there, where
*ther-biforn* previously
*thider* thither, there
*thilke* that, the same
*thinketh* (inf. *thinken*) it
  seems (e.g. *me thinketh*, it
  seems to me)
*thise* these
*tho* those
*thoughte* (inf. *thinken*) it
  seemed
*thridde* third
*thurgh* through
*thurghout* right through
*thyn* thy, thine
*til* to
*to* to, too
*togidres* together
*tombesteres* dancing-girls
*to-night* this last night
*toord* turd
*torente* (inf. *torenden*) torn to
  pieces
*torn* turn
*totere* (inf. *toteren*) tear apart
*traitour* betrayer
*tresor* treasure
*trespas* sin
*trespased* (*to*) offended
  (against)
*trespasse* (inf. *trespassen*) sin
*trete* (*of*) (inf. *treten*) deal
  (with)
*tretee* diplomacy
*trewe* true
*trewely* truly
*treye* three
*triacle* remedy
*troden* (inf. *treden*) stepped
*trone* throne, judgement
  seat
*trouthe* honour

*trowe* (inf. *trowen*) think,
  believe
*tweye* two
*twynne* (inf. *twynnen*) depart
*unbokele* (inf. *unbokelen*)
  unbuckle
*unkindely* unnaturally
*urinals* vessels for holding
  urine
*usage* habit
*useth* (inf. *usen*) practises,
  is addicted to
*vanisshe* (inf. *vanisshen*)
  waste away
*verray* true, real
*vileynye* (ll. 217, 612)
  wickedness; (l. 454)
  rudeness
*wafereres* confectioners
*war* (l. 396 *be war*) beware
*ware yow* (*fro*) (inf. *waren*)
  beware (of)
*warente* protect
*warice* (inf. *waricen*) heal
*weel* well
*welked* withered
*wenche* girl
*wende* (inf. *wenden*) journey
*wende* (inf. *wenen*) (l. 496)
  would have thought
*wenen* believe, imagine
*wey* path, by-way
*whan* when
*whennes* whence
*where* (l. 462) whether
*whilom* formerly, once upon
  a time
*widwe* widow
*wight* person
*wilfully* voluntarily
*winne* (inf. *winnen*) gain
*wise* manner

# Glossary

*wisely* discreetly
*wiste* (inf. *witen*) knew
*wit* wisdom, intelligence
*wives* women
*wol(e)* will, wishes to, desires
*wolde(st)* would(st), wish(est)
*wolle* wool
*wombe* belly
*wonder* extraordinary
*wonne* (inf. *winnen*) gained
*wont* accustomed
*wood* mad
*woodnesse* madness
*woost* (inf. *witen*) knowest
*woot* (inf. *witen*) know(s)
*worm* creeping creature
*worthy* noble
*wrecchednesse* wretchedness
*wrecches* wretches
*wreke him* (inf. *wreken*) avenge himself
*wroghte* (inf. *werchen*) did, made
*wrooth* angry
*wyke* week
*wyn* wine
*wyn-yeving* giving of wine
*wys* wise, discreet
*yaf* (inf. *yeven*) gave

*ybore* (inf. *beren*) born
*ycaried* (inf. *carien*) carried
*ycoined* (inf. *coinen*) coined
*ye* (interjection) yes
*ye* (pronoun) you
*yerne* busily, rapidly
*yet* still
*yeven* give
*yeven, yiven* (inf. *yeven*) given
*yfalle* (inf. *fallen*) fallen
*yfallen* (inf. *fallen*) occurring
*yhent* (inf. *henten*) seized
*yholde(n)* (inf. *holden*) considered
*yiftes* gifts
*ynough* enough
*yow* you
*ypocras* drink of spiced wine
*ypocrisye* hypocrisy
*yset* (inf. *setten*) seated
*yshriven* (inf. *shriven*) confessed
*yslain* (inf. *sleen*) killed
*yslawe* (inf. *sleen*) killed
*ystonge* (inf. *stingen*) stung
*yvele* evil
*ywis* certainly, indeed